Texts, Tea & Tragedy

A Bella Hawkins Mystery

Phylisha Gold

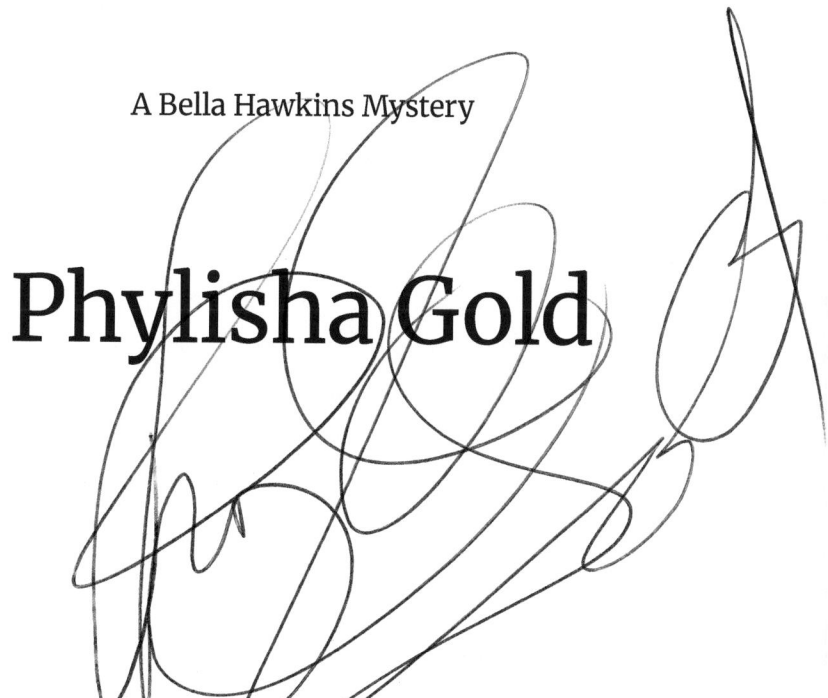

ISBN Paperback 979-8-2186-3803-0

ISBN Ebook 979-8-3492-0920-8

Texts, Tea & Tragedy

This book is printed under the mission and vision of ReSolve Life Coaching by GKA Publishing Group with the sole intent of providing supportive safe entertainment that uniquely and creatively illustrates the wellness strategies that we promote and embrace.

Printed in the United States of America.

Dedication

This is dedicated to all of the butterflies who have shed their shells and finally trusted their wings.

Texts, Tea & Tragedy

Prologue

June 6, 2004. New Orleans, Louisiana.

"This is a beautiful sunset."

"It is."

She wasn't sure that he was actually pursuing her romantically. Sure, they spent a lot of time together and they seemed to have had some things in common, but he never gave her any other reason to think that they were going to be more than friends until recently. Was she crazy to think that this handsome man who was clearly younger than her, could see building a future with her?

"What's wrong?" He asked with a concerned look on his face.

"Why do you think that something is wrong with me?"

"You are so quiet."

"I'm—" She started to lie, but then decided that she might as well tell him what she was thinking. "I guess I am a little confused."

"What are you confused about?" He reached out and held her hand in his.

"Well, I just wish that I knew what you were thinking."

He sat still for a minute as if he was in deep thought. If she didn't know any better, she would have thought that he wasn't even breathing.

"I'm sorry. I just have a lot going on right now." He averted his eyes from hers.

"You want to talk about it?"

"I actually do, but I don't know what that is going to mean for us."

The fact that he used the word us further caused her to believe that she was finally a step closer to the love that she had always wanted. She had had dreams about them being an item and had even fantasized about marrying him one day and having a family, but they had never even kissed. She was forty-three years old and the hopes of having a family of her own was slowly fading away.

"Life has been pretty dark lately. I had given up ever having someone to call my own and to spend the rest of my life with, but then I met you." He shared. There were tears in his eyes.

Her head was full of questions, but she was scared that if she interrupted him, he would not finish what he was saying.

He continued, "My head is all over the place and I know that I have nothing to offer you right now—no home, no title, no future— the only thing that I have right now is my heart." He lifted his head until he was looking deep into her eyes, "is that enough for now?"

She contemplated what he said. She knew that she was not getting any younger and for her to enter into a relationship with this man who was promising her nothing was dangerous. However, if she said no, then might lose any chance at having him in her life and the truth is, she was not strong enough to see what that would be like.

"Yes." She wiped a tear from his cheek.

"Really?" His eyes lit up, his spine lengthened, and he enveloped her hands in between his own. "I thought that this was going to be the last time that I was going to get to be with you."

She took a minute to see beyond the man and hear his heart. She wasn't sure what he was going through, but she was determined to love him through it all. She loved him so much and truly believed that *that* love was going to be enough to get her to her forever.

Chapter One

August 6, 2023, Bedford, Texas.

Unpacking is unsettling. Sure, packing is a feat within itself, but removing the items that had been collected overtime and perfectly fit into spaces designed especially for them while hoping to find a similar home in a new place, is exhausting. Every time that I opened a box, I found myself headfirst inside of it, surprised and annoyed that there was yet more to store away.

I don't like *moving* boxes; they are so troublesome. If I buy them brand new, then I have to assemble them. If I am fortunate enough to find a generous store manager at the nearest dollar store to give me some, then I am blessed. Either way, once the boxes are empty, I still have to decide whether or not to break them down and keep them, or to break them down and throw them out. There is a good argument for both actions: I could keep the boxes just in case I needed to move again, or I could throw them out and get new ones when, or if, I moved again. Needless to say, I don't really like *moving boxes*.

As I finally emptied the last box, I sat in the middle of my new living room. I had left without any furniture, so the apartment was empty. I hadn't wanted to take anything with me because leaving was more important than fighting over who was going to get the toaster. Besides, I quit eating bread about three years ago when my doctor finally figured out that I was allergic to gluten. I couldn't have always been allergic to it. At least I don't think that I was. I honestly do not remember. The last ten years of my life have been like living in a box. There are days that stand out to me, but the rest are different sides of the same box. By the time that I finally decided to get out of the box that was my life, I was left with only feelings.

Feelings. The last thing that I want to do while I am sitting in my new unfurnished space, by myself, is unpack feelings. The thing is—autism is a spectrum and that means no two people on that spectrum will *dys*function the same. There are general truths, but for the most part autism is a garden variety of spicy. For me, having feelings and feeling feelings is a whole ordeal. I cannot not *feel*. Sometimes I feel so much that it renders me dern near comatose. I don't just feel my feelings—I feel everybody's feelings and when my feeling meter is in overdrive, I cannot not fix whatever is broken and that sends me spiraling down into a mental box so deep that I have trouble getting out.

"I'm hungry." I said to myself.

In my brief thought disconnect, it dawned on me that I did not have any food. One of the reasons that I chose this particular apartment was because there was such a variety of businesses that I could walk to. I decided to walk to the little grocery store on the next corner to pick up a few things to sustain me.

While waiting for the light to change, I noticed a man in a brown hoodie and slightly baggy bootcut jeans alone on the other side of the street. While I was trying to discern if he was a threat or not, the light changed. The closer that I got to him, I noticed that he had a goatee with sprinkles of grey and deep set brown eyes that did a horrible job hiding behind unfairly long lashes. Although his hoodie was up, I could tell that he had long locs that were neatly flat-twisted into ropes that rested slightly above his heart. Before I reached his side of the street, I wondered if he was homeless, but as I got closer, I could tell that his style was more artistic than circumstantial.

My mind ran a little rampant about what I should do; cross at a diagonal so I didn't have to pass too close to him or walk past him with an air of indifference. I wasn't scared of him; I just didn't know him and in these days and times, it is always better to be safe than to be sorry.

"It's going to be okay." His voice was low but he held on to each word like the end of a song.

I looked around to see if there was someone else there that I had missed. Plus, I was still not positive that he was not wearing earbuds.

"Are you talking to me?"

He smiled. "You worry too much."

He walked closer to me. I didn't even realize that I had stopped walking.

"Settle your mind. You don't have to figure everything out by yourself." He released a silent laugh that caused his head to nod just a little bit.

That was all that he said to me and then he went back into his own world. I probably should have been more creeped out by that, but when you are a preacher's kid and when you have grown up in the church, having random people walk up to you telling you about you is not that weird.

The evening air was warm, but it also had a cool breeze that lay heavy on my skin like a knitted blanket. The warmth of the evening air coupled with the hints of garlic and curry that swirled around me had no problem reminding me just how hungry I really was.

Usually, I would refrain from deviating from any plan that I created, but then I remembered, this was now *my* life and I could finally do whatever I wanted to do. I did a once over at my clothes and decided that I was dressed well enough to sit inside of a restaurant, so I turned into the shopping center. I let my nose and my curiosity lead me in the search of the smells that drew me out of the way.

The shopping center across from my apartment was just as eclectic as the buildings on the street where I was living, and, I assumed, that was true about the people who chose to call Bedford, Texas home.

I had not met any of my neighbors that lived in my brownstone, but the landlord had told me that, of the four apartments in my building, all of the residents were single and mostly women. The only man in the building was an older Ethiopian man who used to be a professor and whose wife had passed away recently. Across from him was a single mother and her daughter. The older woman and I had the upstairs apartments which also meant that we were fortunate enough to have small balconies. I had rented the apartment sight unseen, but was completely sold on the idea of having an outdoor space. It would be the perfect place for me to read, write, and just be.

My apartment was a one bedroom flat, but I had never been one that wanted to follow tradition. I fully intended on making the bedroom a dressing closet. I planned on using most of the living room area as my bedroom and the dining room as my office. In my mind, I was merely renting spaces and how I chose to use those spaces was completely up to me. I have always been a little quirky, but most people probably do not know that about me. Well, those who *used to* know me were really only those who knew *of* me. I can't say that anyone really *knew* me, because I didn't really know myself. Actually, I still do not, but that is what I am committed to learn.

Finding out who you are is, in its own way, an unboxing. First, you are someone's child and you do what you are told. You go where you are told to go. You wear what you are told to wear. *Then*, when you go to college, the thought is that you are finally in a place where you can explore the world and find out who you are, but the truth is, you just trade one box for another. *Then*, your friends tell you where to go, what to do, and what to wear. *Then*, you get married to someone who tells you where to go, what to wear, and what to do. Somewhere in the middle of all of that, little glimpses of who you truly are peek and peer through the sides of the box until it gets so soggy from your tears that they wear out the tape that's been holding you together.. At that point, there are only two options: crack or crumble.

When I finally reached the door of the restaurant that was responsible for the change in my plans, I attempted to open the door. It was heavy and too difficult for me to get a good grip. Just as the door was about to close again, a tall man ran up behind me and grabbed the door before it closed.

"I got it," he announced over my head. He reached his arm above my head and it was impossible for me to ignore his perfectly sculpted arms peeking out of the sleeves of the white shirt that he was wearing.

"Thank you."

"No problem."

He held the door wide open as the next couple, two young women who appeared to be in the middle of a personal joke of some kind, giggled all of the way to the bar area. They hung lazily onto each other whispering in the other's ear and falling into each other laughing. Both were of similar builds: short, curvy but thin, dark brown and had curly hair. The only real difference, in my quick assessment, was that one seemed to have a strip of green color in her hair. I couldn't hear what they were saying, but I did notice that some of the words were in Spanish.

"Do you want a table or a booth?"

The voice startled me as I was lost in watching how the two women were enjoying each other and being oblivious to everything and everyone one around them. They seemed so free. When I was little, I used to harass my parents about giving me a sibling. I hated being an only child, but it didn't dawn on my small mind that having another child was more difficult than pulling up to the bank and making a withdrawal. It wasn't until I was much older that I considered the quietness that my mother drew across her shoulders after I would ask for a baby sister that I realized that maybe another child was just not possible for them. I had always wanted to have a friend like that. A friend that was so close to me that I could tell all of my secrets to; it would be like a never ending slumber party.

"Would you like a table or a booth?" The voice repeated.

It was the same man who had opened the door. I had been so distracted by the women that I didn't pay any attention to him other than noticing that he was taller and stronger than me. Now that I was taking the time to look at him, I noted that his skin was deep bronze and that made his perfectly white teeth seem to glow. His grey eyes peered both beyond me and somehow also into me.

"A booth is fine." I answered quickly hoping he would not notice that I had been staring at him.

He paused long enough to make me nervous and then he smiled as he tossed a towel onto his shoulder, grabbed a menu from the desk on the side, and gestured for me to follow him. The music made it difficult to think and I struggled following him. I hoped that he would find a place for me somewhere where there was less volume.

As if he had heard my thoughts he said, "I have the perfect spot for you."

I followed him, much like you would follow your parents in a store. The music made it impossible to hear him so I watched his feet as they navigated around sharp corners and dodged busy waiters and excited diners. When he reached a booth that was nestled in the back by the door that opened to the few tables that were on the outside of the restaurant, he stopped and extended his arm and hand and motioned for me to sit down.

"It's perfect, yes?" There was pride in his eyes.

"Yes, thank you."

He let out a little laugh at my automated response. Just as he was about to walk away, he turned back to me and handed me the menu.

"You will need this, yes?"

I nodded and gave the automated smile and laugh that is required to dismiss someone without actually saying that you want them to leave.

After he politely left me alone, I was able to collect my thoughts. I looked around the room; it was nice. Now that I was settled in, the music didn't seem so intrusive, but rather sat in the background and added to the ambience. I placed a napkin over the basket of bread to make sure that I didn't tempt myself.

A couple caught my attention as they were being seated at one of the smaller tables outside. The woman was smiling extra wide and the man was clearly being on his best behavior. They had to be on a first date. There was no familiarity between them. They fumbled as they separated the silverware. There was even a sweet time when they both reached for the butter knife and accidentally touched. I wondered if they would be mad to know that some stranger was witnessing them falling in love. I turned my head to give them some privacy.

"Have you decided what you want to eat?" The man had returned.

"I'm sorry, I haven't even looked at the menu. I got lost in the music, I guess."

"Then it is doing what it is supposed to do. You are new around here, yes?"

I nodded.

"Welcome to Spices and Spirits."

"*Spices and Spirits.*" I repeated.

"The name," he paused while waiting for me to catch a clue and when I didn't, he continued, "of the restaurant."

"I hadn't noticed that when I walked up. I was originally going on a walk and got distracted by the aroma."

"It'll get you everytime. You are forgiven." He scolded with a smile.

"I hope that it tastes as good as it smells."

"Better."

"I can't wait."

"I know that you haven't had a chance to read the menu. Do you mind if I make a suggestion?"

"Not at all–as long as it doesn't have gluten in it."

"I was wondering why you hadn't tried the bread yet.

What happens when you eat gluten? I don't mean to be all up in your business, I have just always wanted to ask somebody."

"Well, different things happen to different people depending on their level of allergic reaction, some people can get sick enough to die."

His look went from curiosity to concern. He sat down across from me and looked intensely into my eyes as I spoke. It made me uncomfortable. Outside of work, I was not used to people listening to what I had to say so intently. I kind of liked it.

"My allergy is not that severe. I bloat and get a really bad stomach ache for a few days. Every once in a while, I might break out in a rash and have excruciating pain in my back and joints." You cannot imagine the horror that filled my spirit after that last word escaped from my mind and trespassed across my lips.

"That sounds horrible!" Surprisingly a flush of concern that was entirely too intense for a stranger, swept his face instead of the justified disgust that I deserved.. "Have you always been allergic? How did you find out?"

I half laughed and half blushed at the speed of his questions. His intrigue seemed so genuine, so innocent.

"I don't think so. I only found out recently—or should I say that I only found out from a doctor, recently."

"That sucks."

"Want to know what really sucks?" I said while slightly recovering from another episode of '*As the Autism Turns.*'

He leaned in and nestled his head on his right hand like he was about to find out the juiciest tea of the day.

"I really, really want to eat this bread."

He exploded in laughter. I found myself laughing with him. I wasn't laughing so much about what I had said as much as I was laughing about *how* he was laughing. He stood up, still wiping his tears, and slid the plate with the bread off of the table and into his hand.

"Not on my watch. Can't have you all bloated and blowing up the bathroom. You might not ever come back."

He walked away and it looked like he was still laughing. I couldn't help but smile. He was a great diversion. I opened up the menu and realized that he never made a suggestion for me to order so I decided to play it safe and order a steak and asparagus spears. I looked into my purse and found the tiny pill bottle of gluten blockers that I keep for those times when I am not so sure if there would be a cross-contamination.

Satisfied that I had finally made a selection, I waited for him to return. I got a little anxious as several minutes went by before I even saw another waiter. I reasoned that the first waiter must have gotten in trouble for spending so much time with me earlier.

"Excuse me, I would like to order now." I called to a young man as he walked by.

The waiter looked at me with a confused look like he didn't understand a word that I was saying. I didn't want to insult him by attempting to figure out what language he spoke, so I just nodded and resigned to wait for the other man to return. About five more minutes went by before I spotted him. He was carrying a plate and headed in my direction. I reached out my hand to stop him as he walked by.

"Excuse me, I'm ready to order now."

He sat the plate down in front of me. It was steak and asparagus spears. I looked up at him in amazement.

"Sorry it took so long. I wanted to prepare it myself to make sure that no one accidentally added flour or anything else that had gluten in it." A sense of pride and protection danced in his eyes

"That was very kind of you, but you shouldn't have done that. I don't want you to get in trouble on my account."

"Don't worry about that. Eat. Let me see how you like it. Don't spare my feelings either. Honesty. Always honesty, ok?"

I picked up the knife and fork and slowly cut the entire steak into bite-sized slices. When I was done, I did the same with the asparagus. I was just about done when I realized that he had sat down in front of me and was waiting patiently for me to try his steak.

"Sorry."

"For what?"

"Cutting my food up before I eat."

"What's wrong with that? I didn't expect for you to pick it up and eat it whole. What's wrong with that?"

He lifted his hand–flapping it quickly to motion for me to hurry and try the steak. Just as I was about to put a fork in the first piece, he stopped my hand. He grabbed the cracked pepper and the pink himalayan salt from the other side of the table and added a little more seasoning to the meat.

"Ok, eat."

I did as invited and was shocked at how perfectly the steak had been seasoned. It melted in my mouth like butter. It was, by far, the most delicious steak that I had ever tasted. I closed my eyes and did a little happy table food dance.

"That's all I needed. I will let you enjoy your meal. I will be back in a little while."

He left me to my plate and I savored each bite like it was my last. It was clear why he could pretty much do what he wanted to do around here. I'm sure the owner knew that he could never replace a chef like that. I ate my food a lot slower than I really wanted to because I just didn't want it to end. I alternately took a bite of the steak and then a bite of the asparagus. I continued this rotation until it was all gone. Begrudgingly, I pushed the empty plate away from me, dabbed my mouth with the napkin and looked back out of the window.

The first couple was gone and had been replaced by another. It was easy to see that this couple had been together for a while. They had history. She was dressed nice enough, but it wasn't overly intentional. He seemed more interested in the game stats that were on the screen behind her. I wondered how long they had been together. They didn't seem much older than me. I could tell that they loved each other deeply, but their love had transitioned from the clumsy, new love that is replete with facades and tempered words into the more settled and secured love that didn't need to be flashy or babied. She didn't care that he was looking at the game stats. She expected that of him. He didn't care that she was reading a book. There would be no arguments about neglect for them. There was enough history of love for them, in their everyday lives, that they didn't need to put it on display in the window of the world watchers for validation or for confirmation.

I knew what that kind of love looked like because that is the kind of love that my parents had. Mom could go to the backyard and curl up in a chair on the patio with a book and Dad could be in his mancave watching football and smoking cigars for hours and neither of them felt slighted or ignored. They respected that they had different interests. They also would sometimes fall asleep in the family room, under one blanket, entangled and intertwined in each other's arms and legs while their favorite movie watched them. They could lay there for hours, sleeping peacefully, as if there was no other place on earth that they would rather be.

I remember the first time that I had seen them like that. I was about thirteen, maybe a little younger. It was the middle of the night, so I had gotten up to get a drink of water from the kitchen. I heard the television in the family room playing, so I walked in and there they were. Of all of the things that I have seen in my life since then, that was and is the one memory that I treasure most.

"Ok, I'm back." The man had returned as promised.

I turned my head slowly to look at the man who had decided to be my companion for the evening. He was handsome and he breathed confidence, comfort, and care. He could have been a model. Although he was a little scruffy, he still looked like he could have been on a men's cologne ad. His jet black hair was cut into a low fade that seemed to melt into his beard. His fingers were perfectly manicured.

"Did you want dessert?" He asked nervously as if he was hoping that I didn't.

"I couldn't eat another bite if I wanted to."

"Good," then he quickly explained, "I'm not saying that it is good that you are full. I don't have anything that you can eat. I have been researching some gluten-free recipes though. I'll have something when you come for dinner tomorrow. Do you like fish?"

"For dessert?" I teased.

"Cheeky rabbit." He joked.

"Yes, I do like fish."

"Good. So tomorrow," His eyes shifted to the ceiling and to the left as he thought. "What about fried catfish, some homemade coleslaw, and some home cut fries?"

"Actually, that sounds amazing."

"And I won't make your plate so full next time. So you can have dessert. Is six thirty a good time for you?"

I laughed before I realized that he was seriously planning dinner for me. "I don't think that I will be back from running errands by then."

"Nine is too late to eat on a weekday. Eight instead, yes?"

I stared at him for a little longer to gauge if he really was being serious. I thought it was a little strange that this man, that I had just met, was making plans for me—more like with me. Typically, I would have been offended, but there was something very protective about him.

"Eight thirty is fine." I looked down at my watch and realized that it was getting late and I still needed to stop by the store before I walked home. "Can I have the check now? It's getting late. I have an early morning and one more stop tonight."

"Where are you going this late?" He squinted his eyes and frowned.

"Excuse me?"

"Tonight. It's getting dark. Is it close?"

"Well, I was on my way to the store on the corner before I came here. I'm just going to pick up some stuff for breakfast."

"Oh, ok, give me a sec." He got up from the table before I could remind him to bring me the check again. When he returned, I was just about to get up so that I could look for someone else to check me out.

"You are ready, yes?"

"Ready?"

"We're going to the store, right?"

"You do not have to walk with me. I will be fine. Besides, aren't you worried about losing your job?"

"I know that I do not *have* to walk with you, I want to. And don't worry about the job, they will be fine."

He extended his hand to help me get up from the table. I scooted to the edge and stood up. His hand was quite a bit larger than mine. I noted how soft his hands were. His long fingers almost wrapped around my hand twice. Once I was sturdy enough to stand on my own, I attempted to release his hand, but he wouldn't let go. He led me back through the maze of waiters and diners and out of the door.

"I still need to pay for my meal," I whispered.

"No, no you don't."

Chapter Two

At first we walked in silence. As we were subconsciously trying to find compatible strides: me with my short slow steps, him with his long fast ones. We were about a block away before we had found our rhythm. He was the first to break the silence.

"Azim."

"I'm sorry, what?"

He didn't turn his head to face me, he only lowered his eyes in my direction. "That's my name. Azim el-Amin Patel."

"Azim? That is a unique name."

"Not in my country." He looked down at me and smiled. "It is actually quite common."

I looked at him again. Never, in any of our interactions, had I thought him anything other than black.

"Your *country*?"

"Morocco."

"I have to admit, I thought that you were an African-American."

"I am. You do know where Morocco is, yes?" He leaned in close to share his juiciest tea, "And I am probably more African-American than you." He smiled. "Amazigh."

"A–a–amah–zigh?" I attempted to say it just as he had done.

He placed his hand on my face and used his fingers to guide my mouth to form the word correctly. "Amazigh."

He repeated it with me. More confident that I could say it by myself, I rehearsed it in my head and then took a deep breath. With an anxious sigh I released the word slowly.

"Amazigh."

"Very good. It roughly translates to *free people*. What is your name?"

"Bella."

"Bella?" He questioned himself as if he was assessing if that name was the name that he would have chosen for me. When he was resigned that it was, he repeated, "Bella. Definitely."

I blushed a little and dropped my head. I didn't think that he would know that it meant beautiful. "How long have you been in America?"

"My parents came here when I was very little–before I was even school age. They made it a point to only speak mainly English at home."

"Do you speak Arabic?"

"Yes but our original language is Tamazight. Only my older family members speak it. My family's travels with my father's business provided a need to know many languages. I learned Arabic, English, and French together."

"Have you been to Morocco? "

"Yes. We still have family there. Actually, *most* of our family is there."

"That is so beautiful. To know where your roots come from. All of that history. It must be a great feeling."

He stopped walking and turned me towards him so that he could look into my eyes. "Your history, here, is not lost to me." He reached out and gently patted the top of my hand. "We are all aware of what the Africans in this country endured. To us, it is you that is amazing."

"Really? I guess it sometimes feels like no one gets it and that no one truly understands how it feels to not know who you are—historically speaking, of course."

"The world is bigger *and* smaller than you think. It is big enough for one to get lost and small enough for one to be found."

I don't know why, but that last statement caused a warm rush to flood my body. Is it crazy to feel so at peace with a perfect stranger? We started walking again.

Now that we were talking, I could hear hints of his heritage. That is the wonderful gift of autism kicking in again and being completely unpredictable. Just as easily as I could find a needle in a haystack, I could also miss a needle in a needlestack. Now that I was paying attention there were slight differences in his syntax. I loved the way he would end a question with a 'yes' or 'no' as if he was seeking some form of validation, but also as a way to encourage me to agree. I wondered if the hints had been there all night and I dismissed them because I thought that he was Black. It's like those pictures that you see on the internet where there are two or more images married into one and the app promises to tell you what kind of person you are by the image that you see first. The dominant side of the brain sees what it wants to see, but once you see the image that you missed, it is almost impossible to see the first image again. Unfortunately, the same is true about people, as well. When you meet someone, you see a world of potential and then when they break your heart, that is all that you can see.

We walked into the store and he immediately led me to the section where there was fresh fruit and vegetables. Pride emanated from him and it was clear that he was very pleased with being my tour guide and took me from one side of the store to the other, grabbing essentials needed for breakfast and late night snacks. On the farthest right side of the store was a glass wall with a door. Even though the lights were off, I could tell that it was most likely a coffee shop that had big comfy overstuffed chairs and walls of shelves filled with books. The sign on the door read *NovelTea*. I made a mental note to visit when it was open.

"You don't need dinner stuff."

"You are right about that. I don't have any pots or pans, yet. To be honest, I don't have much of anything, yet."

"Packed light or packed fast?"

"Light." I said probably too quick to be believable. I didn't feel the need to share, with this stranger, my entire life story. Immediately, I felt guilty about being less than honest. He looked intensely at me, raised one of his thick dark eyebrows and tilted his head slightly.

"That will do," he paused as he smiled, "for now." For the most part, I would have not considered myself the type of woman that would be flustered by a man just because of his looks, but this man was fine and I was having a hard time keeping my distance.

Once we had gotten enough food for a couple of days, we made our way to the counter. There was a woman in line in front of us that was already checking out. She was as brown as me and Azim, but her hair was such a striking shade of blonde that I had wondered if it had been intentional or an unfortunate home dye job experiment gone really wrong.

"Darlin'," She said when she turned to face me, "let me tell you that tea that I got right over there," she pointed to the coffee shop behind me, "sent me all the way back up the Lake Pontchartrain Causeway! Folks just don't know how to make a good cup of sweet tea 'round here. Felt like home on ice."

The woman behind the counter forced a smile with a nervous pride that seemed out of place for the compliment. When she didn't return the banter, the woman looked back to Azim and me as if she was looking for someone that could vouch for Texas's inability to make a good cup of sweet tea.

"Well, I will be back. You don't ever have to worry about not selling that *there* out, no indeed." She looked at us again and then more specifically at me—examining me from crown to toe. "You look like the coffee type."

I was taken aback about her rudeness and was equally irritated because she was absolutely right. I pressed my lips together in the most passive aggressive smile that I could muster and looked up to Azim. He widened his eyes and mimicked my fake smile and communicated through a slight flicker in his eye not to engage. Sensing that she had overstayed her time in the line, the woman took out her card, offered it to the cashier, and walked toward the door. Before she left and as we were moving closer to the register, the woman returned.

"Pardon me again, dollface." She said to the cashier. "I just can't shake it, you look awfully familiar to me. You ever lived in New Orleans?"

"I suppose that I have a common face." The cashier's Spanish accent was so heavy that it made me wonder if she had only recently moved to the United States.

Not completely convinced, but resigned to leave, the woman politely said, "Common is so much better than ordinary. Y'all have a good evening, now."

When the woman walked toward the door, a golden brown dog ran from behind the counter and headed straight towards her growling like the woman had taken her favorite bone. The woman kicked and swung her purse in the dog's direction, but the dog stayed just far enough that the purse could not reach.

"Semper no!" The cashier yelled. Instantly, the dog ran back behind the counter and snuggled against her leg.

"Dogs usually take to me like harmony to a ballad." She smiled at Azim then she sneered at the cashier. "Don't you fret none, that little ol' pooch ain't stopping me from getting my tea."

She turned and finally walked out. I hadn't noticed before, but her presence was so big that it sucked all of the oxygen out of the room. As soon as she left, we all breathed a bit easier.

The cashier was a short woman on the heavier side but definitely not fat by anyone's standards. It was hard to tell how old she was, but I guessed that she was at the very least a decade older than me, if not more. It was difficult to tell because her sienna brown skin was flawless.

While the cashier scanned the items, she occasionally looked up and smiled at us. It was the kind of smile that suggested that she was being let in on a secret.

"Hello Azim. Beautiful lady you got there, mijo." Her words were sprinkled with hints of mothering that made her voice very comforting.

He looked at me as if it was for the very first time, but it made me feel like he had done it for a lifetime, "Yes, she is."

"That will be $54.71." She said through a crooked smile that was failing to restrain a knowing laugh. I retrieved my card from my purse and attempted to insert it in the machine, but was met with a very light tap on the back of my hand and a very slight head shake of disapproval. Azim stepped closer and inserted his card, entered his pin, and took the receipt from the lady. I stared at him and he pretended not to feel the heat of my gaze.

"Mija, when a good man wants to buy you things," she shrugged and threw out her hand to either side of her, "you let him."

I waved to her as we left the store and walked back towards the direction of the restaurant.

"You have to be the best welcome wagon in history. I appreciate you for all that you have done, tonight, but I must be getting on home."

Azim stopped walking. There was another look of disappointment in his eyes that puzzled me. Did he think that I was going to invite him back to my apartment? I had already been way too friendly with this stranger and that was neither smart nor safe.

"You sound as if we are not going to see each other again. You are still coming for dinner, yes?"

I felt slightly obligated to agree to meet him for dinner. I didn't know if I wanted to feel obligated to meet with anyone, especially a man. Not again and not so soon.

Chapter Three

As an English professor, it is easy to find teaching positions so moving has never been difficult. Being an educator has also afforded me the freedom to seek other types of positions where my specific skill set was beneficial and not be tied down to office spaces, office gossip, office parties, or anything else that comes with being in an office. I can teach and go home. It's not that I don't like people, I just like my freedom more. Freedom has been an expensive commodity for me and I just was not ready to give it up. When I had finally gotten sick and tired and tired of being sick, I bolted.

Being a professor is not exactly how I had envisioned my writing career developing. In my dreams, I was a novelist. Not just any kind of novelist; I wanted to tell universal stories that would not be stereotyped and thrown into a category just because of the color of my skin. If there is one thing that I have found out in life, it is that love, war, and everything in between, is relational, conditional, and most importantly universal. In retrospect, I realized that who I am is always going to color the lenses of my experiences. There is no way for me to extricate *me* from my writing just to appeal to a larger audience. But why should I have to? Why should I even have to contemplate muddying the literary waters with ambiguous banter that absolves and utterly erases the uniqueness and diversity of the black experience? I shouldn't. Being a black person is not a monolith. The problem is that my experience is not, for many, black *enough*. I could never write about the compartmentalized stories of some who share my race because I would have no point of personal reference. Am I saying that somewhere in my family there isn't someone in jail or on drugs? No. However, isn't that true about *all* families? Am I proclaiming that there isn't one single mother working a dead-end job and struggling to keep the lights on and her legs closed? No. Yet again, that is not a scenario that escapes *any* race, color, or socioeconomic status. It is what it is. I just don't want to write about it. It is not my experience and I was not willing to exploit anyone experiencing that just to sell a story that is edgy and confirms, for some, what being black in America is all about.

The one person that I knew who could probably pull off writing a novel like that was my white friend, Leah. She would say and do just about anything. She was built like the baby of a brick house and a stallion and could *easily* have become a model. In school, she was the fire in our little group; it was just Leah, Thuy, and me. I can't tell you how many times that I had to pray us out of some mess that her mouth got us into. I envied that about her though. It wasn't until much later and after we had lost touch with one another that I found out *why* she was the way that she was.

She was the oldest of three children. Her parents had broken up and it was a messy kind of breakup. Her father didn't just leave the house, he left their lives totally. The pressure was so much that it caused her mother to crack mentally and she spent most of Leah's teenage years in and out of mental health hospitals. By the time Leah was in college, she had full custody of her siblings—one of which had down syndrome.

It was maybe six years ago when I ran into Leah at the mall. She was still drop-dead gorgeous, but the light that had been living in her eyes was gone. She now had her own children and was coping the best way that she could. I begged her to sit with me in the food court and to let me treat her to lunch.

March 3, 2017 Edmond, Oklahoma.

"Your babies are so beautiful, Leah. They look just like you. How is your mom?"

"Your guess is as good as mine, girl. Remember when we were in college and I had to move back home because they were putting her away?"

"I do. I thought it was only temporary."

"It was supposed to be, but just like my mother, she decided that she knew what was best and she broke out of the hospital. No one has seen or heard from her since."

"Oh my dear Lord! Is that how you got custody of your brother and sister?"

"Girl, that and a thousand other reasons. It was ok, though, because nobody was going to take my kids away from me. Hell, I was the only real mother that they really knew anyway."

"That was a heavy load for someone so young. It's nothing but the grace of God that you—" I stopped before I completely inserted my foot into my mouth.

"Didn't lose my mind?" She finished my thought.

"I'm sorry. I didn't mean to be insensitive."

"I ain't trippin'. You know me. The one thing I do best is keep it pushing."

"Kaylee should be in her mid-twenties, right?"

"Twenty-six next month.'

"Are you freaking kidding me? How in the world is that even possible?"

"Crazy ain't it?"

"What about Bobby?"

Leah looked off to her daughter and retrieved a toy that she had thrown out of the stroller.

"Bobby died a few years back."

"Leah! Why didn't you tell us? We would have been there for you. I am so sorry!"

"Life has always been life for me. Bobby dying and my mother running off is what it is. I didn't choose this life, it fell in my lap, so *what* did Leah do?"

"Kept it pushing." I recalled her favorite saying. "What about now, are you married?"

"Helllllllll naw, girl. That is not even on my bucket list." Looking down at my engagement ring, "Y'all can have all that. I'm good."

"You have always said that. Well, I hope their father is at least helping you raise these cuties."

"These ain't *my* kids, these are Kaylee's. I raised her and Bobby and now, most of the time, I am raising hers, too."

"Oh Leah, what about you? I mean, what are you doing for you?"

"I go to work and I take care of my grandchildren."

I looked at this beautiful friend of mine and I became deeply ashamed. I should have been there for her. I could have helped her out. She was right; this has always been her life and truth be told, why would she have called me?

"Here, give me your phone. I am going to put my number in it and I want you to call me. Matter of fact, I'm calling my phone from yours so that I can get your number. We are going to do something this weekend if it is nothing but take the kids to the zoo."

"I would like that." She smiled.

For the first time since we started talking, I saw a glimmer of light behind those big gray eyes.

I kept my promise and we took the kids to the zoo that weekend. We had so much fun! I made another promise to be a better friend and to keep up with her. Weekends became our thing and it seemed to really lighten the load for Leah. I was in awe of her and all that she endured.

We had been going out for about six months and had finally planned a vacation without the kids when Leah called me frantic.

"Sis, I hate to even ask you to do this."

"Whatever it is, you know I'm there."

"Can you come over and stay with the kids for a little bit? Kaylee was supposed to be home, but she hasn't made it yet."

"Is everything alright?"

"I'm not sure. I hope that she is not with they daddy."

"Surely she wouldn't go back over there."

"That's that love shit I be talking about. Y'all can have it."

"What are you going to do?" I was becoming concerned. Leah had a history of hitting first and asking questions later.

"I'm going to drive over there and see if she is there. I can't stop grown folks from doing what they want to do, but if she is over there, she is going to have to stay over there."

"Ok, I'm on my way."

When I got to Leah's house, she was standing on the porch smoking a cigarette. I didn't even know that she smoked.

"Are you sure that you want to go over there?" I asked as I walked up to the door.

"Shit, I don't have much of a choice."

"Is he dangerous?"

"Not half as dangerous as I am. Besides I am not going in, I'm just driving by."

"Ok, but you call me as soon as you get there. As a matter of fact, you call me before you get on the street."

"Ok, girl." She laughed knowing that there would be nothing that I could have done to help.

I closed and locked the door after I heard Leah pull off. She had always been so gangster. I said a quick prayer that she would keep the gangster in tonight or maybe just let out the baby gangster at bare minimum.

I sat for about an hour before I called her phone. I didn't know where she was going, but I did know that she should have been there by now. The phone rang at least seven times before it went to voicemail. I hung up and called back; each time the phone rang seven times before it went to voicemail. I was beyond afraid and began yelling at myself for not at least getting the address. It was only when the bright lights from a car outside shone in the window that I realized that I had worried myself to sleep. I jumped up and ran to the door–fully expecting to see a police car. However, when I opened the door, I was still surprised that there was actually a police car there and an officer was walking to the door.

"Officer, what happened?" looking behind him and waiting for an answer I urged, "Where is Leah?"

"Are you Bella?"

"Yes, I am. Where is Leah? Is she ok?"

"Can you step outside?"

"I have two babies here and I don't want to leave them in the house alone. Can you please tell me where Leah is and if she is ok?"

"Give me just a minute."

The officer walked back to the car and bent down to speak to someone. The passenger car door opened and another officer got out. This officer, a female, walked up to me. Her demeanor was less serious.

"Ma'am. I was told that there are children in the residence?"

"Yes."

"Would you mind me staying right here at the door while you step to the police car for a moment?"

"I gu–guess that would be ok."

The walk to the car was indeed the longest walk that I had ever taken. When I finally got to the first police officer and the car, I attempted one more time to get him to tell me what was going on.

"Officer, I must admit that you are scaring me. Can you please tell me if my friend Leah is ok?"

He opened the door to the backseat and Leah was there laying down.

"What's wrong with her?"

"She witnessed her daughter being shot by her boyfriend. She rushed to her and took her to the hospital. I am sure that she was acting in a state of shock and on autopilot."

"Oh my Lord! Is Kaylee okay?"

"I'm sorry ma'am. She didn't make it. Ms. Andrews was in no condition to drive home so we brought her. Her car is still at the hospital."

"Did you catch him?" Anger and fear filled my face.

The officer looked at me longer than I thought he should have, then he adjusted his gaze.

"The suspect didn't run ma'am." He darted his eyes towards Leah to let me know that he was censoring what he was saying in front of her. "He was still at the house when the officers arrived." Then he whispered, "Self-inflicted."

I looked at Leah laying there so broken and vulnerable. I had never seen her like that. I asked the officer if I could approach the car and help her out. He nodded and helped me. Leah's legs were like jello. Her eyes were swollen almost completely shut. Her hair was matted and tangled. With Leah being so much taller than I, the officer had to do most of the lifting; I basically carried her purse in. He had no problem lifting her. He was taller than Leah. He was probably about six foot six. His uniform was not a tight fit, but it also did a horrible job hiding his muscles.

We got her in the door and to the couch. The officers offered their condolences again and promised that if there was anything that they could do, they would and we should just call them directly. The male officer handed me his card.

"Please call if you need anything."

"Thank you."

I closed and locked the door behind. When I turned and looked at Leah, she was sitting up staring into space.

"Honey, do you want something to drink? Some tea?"

"No, thank you," she responded without looking at me, "You know," she began still not looking at me, "the love of a sister is sometimes stronger than a mother's."

I didn't know what to say to that. I've always had my mother and I didn't have any siblings. "Do you mind if I stay here with you for a while?"

Still not looking at me she whispered, "I would like that. Thank you."

"Why don't you go and take a shower. I will make you some tea. It will be right by your bed. Is there anything else that I can get for you?"

"No, I don't think so."

I had never helped someone prepare for a funeral then and truth be told, I didn't know how anyone made it through it. How heart wrenching it was to watch Leah pick out a dress and a casket for her daughter who was really her sister. All I knew was that she did not deserve this. She didn't deserve any of this. Not one moment of her life was fair. The children that she raised, without complaint, were gone. Her whole life had been about them. And now? Now, she wasn't even going to get a chance to see what life could be because she would be forever tied to her grandchildren who were really her niece and nephew.

I tried my best to maintain our friendship, but I think Leah was just too hurt and her heart was just too broken to love anyone outside of those babies. It wasn't long before she stopped answering my calls. I didn't know what to do other than let her feel what she was feeling and not become another burden on her. It was about a year later when I ran into her again at the same mall and almost in the exact same place. I was so happy to see her! I ran to her and extended my arms for a hug and she politely pulled away. I won't lie, it kind of shocked me. She looked at me, square in the eyes, and silently pleaded for me to let her just be. What could I do? So, I watched my best friend turn around and walk out of my life forever.

See, that is the kind of story that the publishers wanted me to write; the only problem was that it wasn't my story and she wasn't black.

Chapter Four

I may not have had that kind of story, but I would be lying if I said that I didn't have one. Moving wasn't really a choice for me as much as it was required for me to actually be able to live. I was not being threatened nor was I dying from some mysterious disease. I just needed to get away from everything and everybody. I needed a new life because the one that I had had betrayed me.

I hate to seem as though I am going to go off on the stereotypical tangent about a failed relationship that was replete with lies, sex, and videotapes. It was not. I mean there were no videotapes that I know of.

I pride myself on being the type of person that no one has to lie to. I am not the kind of person that has a tight grip on the rules and regulations of life so much so that I cannot understand that life is made up of split-second choices. By no means am I presenting myself as obligatory to the void of having a moral standard, I just know that I have not always made the right choices and I give others the space to grow. I only have ONE rule: DO NOT LIE TO ME.

At least that is who I think that I am. Marcus and I had had good times and the good was definitely more impressive than the bad. My mother, from the onset of our marriage, had told me that all relationships go through rough times, so I tried to be like my mother—positive. Marcus was not a *bad* man; he was a great guy, actually. He supported me when I first started writing. He came to all of my events and he had copies of all of the books or journals that carried my stories, but he never read them which made me wonder why he wanted them. Maybe that was it—he wanted to look like the perfect guy for me, but when we were at home, alone, he wasn't.

When the inevitable conversation came about marriage while we were dating; he didn't propose to me, he just told me to pick a date. It was, by far, the most unromantic coupling ever. In hindsight, I guess *that* should have been a red flag. As we moved closer and closer to the date, I was more *afraid* of it than I was *excited* about it. Each day, I looked at him hoping that he would turn to me and call it off, but he didn't. Of course that was easier said than it was going to be done because I didn't know what the truth was. I was not in love with this person. I thought that I was and I was sure that if we just kept going, I would somehow fall in love, but *something* just wasn't right. I felt horrible. Venues were being rented. Clothes were being selected. Flights and hotel rooms were being reserved and there was something deep down in my soul that was telling me to run.

Leading up to the wedding, I didn't go out much at all and I didn't answer the telephone. I didn't have many friends—just Thuy and Leah and both time and life had distanced us, so I was reduced to asking colleagues to be bridesmaids because I didn't know enough people in my personal life to match with the hundreds of groomsmen he had. Ok, there were not hundreds, but he definitely had more friends than I did. As a point of contention between us, he had so many friends that it often felt like he didn't have time for me. Sure we went to dinner and to the movies, but we rarely did anything that I was interested in and since he was just about to make partner at his law firm, it became increasingly important for me to attend all of their events. I started to feel like a prop.

When we would get to the events, he would sit me down in a corner somewhere and then he would be off with the other lawyers. Don't get me wrong, I could hold my own in any room, I just didn't understand why I was there if he didn't actually want to be with me. We never danced together. We didn't do the "couple flirting," I was just there.

About a year and a half into our marriage, I was out shopping for a dress to wear to one of his firm's functions when my head started thumping like it had a heartbeat. The beating got louder and louder until I passed out. When I woke up in the hospital, the doctor told me that my blood pressure was extremely high, so I would need to stay in the hospital overnight or until they could get it back to a healthy place. Once my mother found out that I was in the hospital, she planted herself next to my bed and did not move until I was released. That was my mommy; she was perfect.

August 27, 2019, Edmond, Oklahoma

"Mommy," I had whispered in between tears, "I can't keep doing this. How do I tell him?"

She looked at me deeply and said, "Tell him the truth."

Of course that was easier said than it was going to be done because I didn't know what the truth was. I was not healthy, but I was also not in love with this person.

When I got out of the hospital, I made it a point to stay home. I didn't go out much at all and I didn't answer the telephone . The medication that the doctor gave me was doing wonders for my blood pressure and the therapy seemed to be doing wonders in other areas. In one of my last sessions, my therapist asked me the same question that she asked me when we first met.

"What is really wrong?"

When she asked me before, I couldn't answer her, but over the weeks and through my journaling, I had identified a lot of things that were wrong.

"I want to be married, but not to *him*. I don't trust him, and I do not know why. "We don't talk much. At first, we would laugh ourselves to sleep, but after we got married, the laughter stopped. He started treating me as something that he *had* to have as opposed to being someone that he wanted to have. Sure, we had fluffy dialogues about what to eat, where to go, what to watch, but we never talked about our hopes and dreams. Then he started complaining about how I didn't mingle with the other wives. I've always been the person that I am, but he wanted me to be," and as if a light had come on, I said, "someone else."

"Our spirit knows things that our brains have to learn. Trust it."

When I left the session, I was determined to tell Marcus that we should get a divorce. I didn't know how he would respond, but at this point, I didn't care. When he got home we were going to have the hardest conversation of our relationship. When I got home, his car was in the driveway, so I drove my car to the back and put it in the garage. I was a little shocked that he was at home so early, but reasoned that this was even better because I would not have time to talk myself out of it.

I opened the door, put down my keys, cell phone, and purse in the kitchen and headed to the bedroom. I looked around the house, but he was not there. I walked back to the kitchen to grab my phone when he opened the front door. He didn't see me because he and his friend Donte were frantically ripping each other's clothes off while they were kissing violently. I didn't move. I didn't make a sound. I just stood there watching my husband make out with his best friend. Before it could get to the place of no return, I whispered,

"Marcus?"

Marcus tapped Donte on the top of his head and nodded in my direction. No lies could be told because they were naked and Donte was kneeling down in front of Marcus. I didn't wait to hear anything and I asked no questions. I grabbed my things and walked out of the door for good.

Marcus called my phone so much that I had to turn it off. I didn't want to speak to him. I just needed to get somewhere quick and make sure that I didn't have a freaking stroke. There was only one place that I wanted to be and that was laying in my mommy's lap.

I didn't have to tell her anything. She saw it in my face. I never knew if it was her intuition or that discernment that my mother was always encouraging me to tap into. She told me repeatedly to 'try the Spirit by the Spirit' and then trust it. That was about as preachy as my mother would get with me. Even though both of my parents were pastors, neither of them ever treated me like I was one of the members in the congregation and they never let any of the church folk treat me like it either. They were quick to tell me that I had to get to 'know the Lord' for myself. I had to admit, I wasn't very good at it. I considered myself a believer, too. There just seemed to be too many rules for me. Too many don'ts. Which was crazy because I didn't do anything. I didn't *do* anything not because I felt convicted, but because I just didn't want to and I didn't have much reason to think that others who *'sinned'* were bad people. I just figured everybody was trying to figure life out and that just made us human. No matter how much I skirted the church, people seemed to be drawn to me because of it and I was still trying to find out where I fit in.

My mother told me that I was gifted. I am pretty sure that all good mothers tell their children that. I do not think that Leah's mother ever told her that and I know for certain that Thuy's mother was never around long enough to tell her that.

I was about five years old when I was diagnosed with autism. That was my gift, my mother told me. She told me that God had given me a brain that was flexible and a spirit that was powerful and that I was going to be able to see things that others would not and know things that others could not. Neither of my parents ever made me feel like there was something wrong with me, but they did have to learn how to deal with my anxieties and emotional meltdowns. I am definitely sure that it was more than challenging having to answer my millions of questions over the years while giving me my space to be alone in my own quiet to find answers on my own.

I loved being alone. I liked hiding inside of my head. Now, do not get me wrong, I also desired to have people in my life, it was when I got overstimulated that I needed a safe and quiet place to go and put my puzzles together by myself.

I have been putting puzzles together all of my life. When I was a little girl, I would hide away with my puzzles and did not want to be disturbed, eat, sleep, or drink. If the puzzle had a butterfly on it, well, let's just say that would have been the perfect way to kidnap me.

I switched from puzzles to mysteries my senior year in high school. Leah, Thuy, and I were always finding some way of getting into non-trouble, trouble. Thuy was *man crazy*. I don't remember her ever being without a boyfriend, but there was usually something wrong with them.

Friday, May 29, 1993, Norman, Oklahoma

Right before we graduated from high school, Thuy had broken up with Jeremy, one of the best basketball players in the school so we had to do something to cheer her up. Someone had told us that there was going to be a party in Norman at the university. So what did we do? We snuck out of course. My mother thought that I was at Thuy's house. Thuy's mother thought that she was at my house but in reality, we were at Leah's house completely unsupervised. Since her mother was never there even when she was, we had the car at our disposal. That was one of the rare occasions that Leah's mother was actually taking care of her own kids.

When we got to the party, the music was loud and there were so many people there that I started spiraling from the overstimulation. None of my friends knew that I was autistic at the time; I was the master masker. So when they hit the dancefloor, I found a dark corner and hid with my fingers in my ears until a fight broke out. The fight unlocked another fear that was bigger than the noise, so I found Leah and Thuy and stayed on their heels until we left. When we were outside, we stood around, like everybody else. Before we left, a guy walked up to Thuy and started talking to her. He was only able to give her his name before gunshots rang out. He took off running; we did, too. When we finally got to Leah's car, Thuy was devastated because she had decided that she was now in love with Shawn.

The following week, all we heard about was how fine he was and how she needed to find him. So I did. I put my gifts into action and before the end of the week, I knew his last name, his occupation and location, his telephone number, and where he lived. I did all of that before the internet was really a thing!

After that, I became the friend who did those kinds of things. I could find anything and anyone. I could figure out anything and I would not go to sleep until I did. My love for puzzles moved out of boxes and into my head.

Even though I could seemingly figure out the most complex problems, simple things had a tendency to elude me, but once I saw it, I could never unsee what I saw and I just added it to my cognitive library of stuff that most people didn't know or care about. So, when I found out that husbands could cheat, that is all that I saw.

August 30, 2019, Oklahoma City

Mom held me and didn't attempt to let me go until I moved first. She was amazing like that. I don't know what I would do without both of my parents. They have always pushed me to see what the limits were. Most of the time, I found out that there were none. Usually, being with my mother would have fixed it all, but for some reason, that was not the case this time. I got away from everyone. I had to.

When I had finally gathered myself and had cried all of the tears that I was going to give that man, I told my mother that I had been offered and had accepted a job at the university where Thuy worked. Neither my mother nor my father tried to stop me; I definitely thought that they would because I felt like I was running away.

"Dad, are you disappointed that I am moving?"

"Disappointed, in you? Never. Love you and will miss you? Always."

He hugged me tightly and promised to help me pack. I didn't want much from the house, so that went rather quickly. Everything had too many feelings attached, so I only took the barest of essentials and decided to truly start over.

Chapter Five

The next morning, I got up earlier than usual. I was always the first person to wake up in my family. I love the mornings because the whole world is still asleep—well except for me, the birds, and the criminals. Actually, considering how early that I get up, they are probably still asleep, too. It's a common misconception that most crime is committed at night, but when you factor in all of the white collar and political crimes that happen daily, I suspect that that trope is more likely to be false. Crimes occur when there are opportunities and 'no other choices.'

I personally do not think that most crimes are planned, well, not in the traditional sense. I think that some people find themselves in places where their lack of choices have guided them and then they think that there is only one option left. Of course there is always the option of not doing the wrong thing, but when we are controlled by our innermost desires, we do whatever we can to ensure that those desires are not just met but are as protected as they can be.

Sometimes, we find ourselves at the mercy of other people's choices and our life's paths are altered. That is, of course, why I am here in Bedford trying to make a new life. That is also why I have been sitting here for two hours trying to convince myself that this new life and this new job is going to work out for me. I must admit that I had never thought that I would ever live in Texas. I had visited many times before and all I could remember was that I could not imagine having to fight with that kind of traffic every day, but Bedford was different. It did not seem to even be a part of Texas. Most places that are needed daily are within walking distance. It felt safe; it felt like home. As I could best assess, the only place that I really had to drive to was work and I really didn't have to do that either because this college town was kind enough to have free public transportation that was clean *and* that went right to the university.

I decided to sit outside on my balcony for a while, drink my coffee, and listen to the wind. At this time in the morning, that was all that I could hear. I was the only one awake and I loved it. Now, do not get me wrong, I was not going to be walking around town at this time of the morning alone, but I also did not feel like I couldn't do so if I wanted to.

As soon as the sun came up, I knew that that was my cue to get ready for work. I had left all of the things for my office in my car when I moved in, so I did not have to worry about that. My first day would most surely be about meeting my colleagues, walking around campus, and settling in. I had not physically met the English department chairperson yesterday when I completed the onboarding, but I had had the opportunity to sit with the Vice President of Academic Affairs, Dr. Abebaw and I instantly adored him.

When I arrived on campus on my first day, Dr. Abebaw came out of his office like he had been waiting for my arrival. Every step that he took had a distinct purpose about them. His pace wasn't particularly slow; however he was not in a hurry either. When he finally reached where I was, I didn't have to do much to adjust my eyes to meet his. Once he was settled in my presence, he politely placed his hands behind his back in a manner that let me know that this was his natural habit. It was clear that he was quite a bit older than me, but his eyes had both a youthful gaze and a depth of wisdom that permeated past words or protests. His deep mahogany skin held an uninterrupted history deeper than my own and had just enough light in it that allowed for his weathered features to be seen. His presence was sure, but his company was kind. He was handsome in the kind of way that you could tell that your grandfather was. He looked at me in the slightest of pauses, nodded his head, smiled, and let out the quickest of giggles. It was so slight that if I had been distracted by his appearance, I would have missed it.

"Ahhhhhh, Dr. Hawkins." He exhaled and held onto the last note of his greeting.

"Nice to see you again, Dr. Abebaw." I extended my hand and was preparing to give him my practiced firm shake of confidence and authority but before I could, he took my hand and placed one of his on the bottom and one on the top and gently gave it, what I can only describe as a hand hug.

"It is very nice to see you. Please. Come."

I looked at the receptionist and she smiled. I don't even think that I had noticed her when I walked in. I don't typically overlook people. I make it my mission to acknowledge every person that I meet so that they feel seen. I made a mental note to remember to send her a quick note once I settled in.

I followed Dr. Abebaw to his office. It was not overrun with decor and it was not as spacious as most Vice

President's offices. The few pieces of furniture that were there were very old, very well cared for, and very heavy.

"Please, do what you need to do to become comfortable."

I expected him to invite me to sit down, but when he said that, I instantly became uncomfortable. When my Autism and ADHD collide, making decisions based on how *I* feel when I have not created a mental Vinn diagram to identify my feelings, is not an easy task. I decided to sit down, not because I wanted to but because it was, by far, the easiest thing to do.

"Dr. Hawkins, I have had the privilege of reading some of your poems and short stories. I would like to take this time to celebrate you."

"Ummmmm, thank you," I stammered out.

His dedication to being intentional made me nervous. It wasn't a cringy type of feeling, but it did make me be extremely careful with my word choices. When you're a masker, you become very skilled at reading other people's emotions and basing your behavior and responses off of what you perceive that they will find most helpful or pleasing. Overtime and as I had gotten older, it became quite maddening to constantly have to be in tune with the world around me and having to listen to the thousands of voices giving me directions and suggestions. So as much as I adored how Dr. Abebaw used his words with purpose, I now had the added chore of assimilating this into my long list of things to do to look normal.

Some of the voices in my head are louder than others and help me to get through the minutiae of the day. My mom's voice is the most prevalent. She has a way of pushing me and guiding me that doesn't force me to be a carbon copy of the world that swirls around me. My mother's voice reminded me that 'life and death are in my mouth' so I should be very careful about what I say. Do I *always* adhere to that, absolutely not. Did I mention that self-regulation is a struggle?

When I was younger, I would blurt out whatever I was thinking whenever I was thinking it. People would be so angry with me and I would be so confused. Besides, what had I really done wrong? I had only told the truth. I quickly learned that the majority of people that I had encountered did not find solace in the truth and they definitely did not want that truth coming from a human lie detector. After many awkward situations and failed friendships later, I learned to harness that power and cover it with a plush, cozy blanket of indifference.

Each time that I would find myself in a situation that my mouth and my curiosity had gotten me into, my mother would pat my hand and say, "Your kind of truth brings the kind of light that shatters darkness. Some people would rather be blind and in the dark, so be mindful of how you share your light."

Although I had only just met him, I felt like Dr. Abebaw was a lot like my mother.

"You will be a good fit here. You will bring order and that order will bring peace." He interrupted my thoughts.

"Dr. Abebaw, I have to admit that I am a little overwhelmed right now. I probably should tell you that I am—I have ASD."

He smiled. " We leave small places because it is important to have space to grow. If you cannot grow, you cannot live to your fullest potential. You are you, just in a bigger place." He tilted his head slightly peering into my eyes for understanding. "Let us take a walk around the campus. I want you to see, hear, and" he placed his hand on his heart, "know." His eyes found mine again and then he simply nodded and then stood up. "Then, I will take you to your building."

As we walked, I didn't feel the need to say much of anything and Dr. Abebaw didn't speak much either. Should I have explained to him what ASD was? Why did I assume that he would know anything about Autism? After many minutes of second and third guessing myself, I finally quieted my mind and listened to the sounds of the campus.

When we crossed paths with someone who he knew, he would stop, introduce us to each other and then tell them something personal for which he celebrated them. I wondered if he did that all day—every day. My mind went down that rabbit hole that it always does, and I began to fake calculate how many times he must have had to do that in a day. Before I arrived, I found out—ok, I didn't just find out. I went down the hyper-fixated research rabbit hole and learned that he had been with the university for over thirty years, so if he had taken the time to celebrate everyone that he knew——he must have said that thousands, if not millions, of times!

We arrived in front of a building that seemed to have more glass than anything else. A woman wearing a scarf around her head and tied under her chin, stopped us. She was what the church ladies would have called *pleasantly plump*. That probably was not a socially correct way of saying that, but it was in my head and it made me smile.

"Good morning, Dr. Bisson. I celebrate you for the colorful way that you fill the world with words."

Dr. Bisson ceremonially bowed her head slightly while daintily placing her hand on her more than generous chest and said, "I will never not love hearin' that Dr. Abebaw." She turned to look at me as if she had not noticed that I was standing there, "Don't you just love him? I don't think we have met. I'm Dr. Chaitra Bisson. I'm new here—well at the university obviously. Clearly I am anything but new."

She laughed again. This woman was a living, breathing, Blanche Deveraux. That slow southern drawl juxtaposed with her dark Indian features and poorly hidden platinum blonde hair made for a walking museum of visual complexities and delight. Her suit was as tight as it was short and matched her high heels perfectly. I instantly knew that she was the same woman that was at the corner store.

I smiled, "Nice to meet you. Dr. Abebaw was escorting me around the campus. Today is my first day as well."

"Really?" She said with a hint of disbelief that she did not bother trying to hide. "Now if that don't just put the hinky in ya dinky!"

I laughed not because I was unaware that she was shocked that I was a professor, but rather because I had seen characters on screen that said things like that, but I had never once, in real life, met someone who actually did it.

"Dr. Bisson, this is Dr. Hawkins." Dr. Abebaw proudly interjected. "Dr. Bisson is in our psychology department. She brings a wealth of knowledge in neuropsychiatry learning and its effects on children of color."

This statement bothered me and excited me to my core, so I slipped deeper into my professional mask. I am pretty sure that my attempt to be interested while appearing to be unconnected to the subject matter was not successful.

"Well just spill all of my goodies then Dr. Abebaw!" She winked at me and leaned in closer to me, "Heck if you are doing what *we* do, you gotta have a little something divergent in there somewhere, right?"

I smiled awkwardly. Could she tell that I was autistic or was she just being funny?

"Dr. Hawkins is in our English department. She is an award winning author and poet."

"A doctor and a writer?" She almost sang. "Good for you! Who says that affirmative action doesn't work! Honey, we are going to have to get together sometime. I got a story about a case of this little girl that I was working on back home in New Orleans that will for sure get you a best seller! Do you write true crime?" She asked without giving me an opportunity to respond. "You should."

I don't often share that I am a writer because once people find out, they almost always have a story for me that will be sure to get me a best seller. "We will have to schedule some time to have a chat." I said knowing that I would never do so.

"I have been waiting to tell some of the stories of home." For just a moment, I sensed a bit of sadness in her. "It was a difficult time after the passing of my dear husband. We weren't fortunate enough to have children so I spent some time working with them." A small bell rang and she looked down at her watch, "Well, I'm going to get on along my way now. 'Sposed to be going to this committee meeting. Look at me. I ain't been here a good week and I done already signed up to be all up in folks' projects. Dr. Hawkins, you come on over to the psyche building anytime that you want. I might have left Louisiana, but baby she right here with me. I always have something to smack ya lips on. And can't nobody do sweet tea like I do sweet tea."

With that, she turned and literally sashayed down the sidewalk. I had never seen anyone sashay, but believe me when you have been in the presence of the woman that was Chaitra Bisson, you knew that you had been truly sashayed by the finest.

Chapter Six

A few more steps, brief encounters with students, yard workers, and faculty later, we had reached the Humanities building. Even though the building was also mostly glass, I could not actually see into it. I wondered if it had the opposite effect in the evening. Once we entered, I was pleased to see how many students were hanging around, talking, and reading. I don't remember students hanging around our building when I was in college. I think that we tried to get as far away from the point of pain as possible, but these students really seem to be enjoying their space. It was busy but not loud. There were even a few students who were clearly asleep.

The space where the professors' offices were was very spacious. I suppose that it would have to be considering that there were so many of us. Core subjects with majors always have the most faculty. No student is safe from an English class once they make it on campus. When we entered the department suite, I made it a point to speak to the receptionist because I still felt bad about not doing so when I was in the Vice President's office earlier.

"Hello, I'm Bella Hawkins, the new English professor." My introduction was both a statement and a question because I was always fearing that something bad would happen.

"Nice to meet you Dr. Hawkins. I have heard so many good things about you. We are all glad that you are joining our family."

"Thank you, I really appreciate that. What is your name?"

"Crissy."

"It is very nice to meet you Crissy and I look forward to working with you." I refrained from telling her that she could just call me Bella. When I first became a professor, I regularly told everyone to just call me by my first name, because I noticed that a lot of my male colleagues throughout the years had had no problem with students addressing them by their first names. Unfortunately, it just doesn't seem to work out for female professors. That level of familiarity undermined the already thin amount of respect given to women and my first name quickly became, "baby girl," "girl," "fren," or whatever new term that was floating around. I also maintained a very professional appearance because casual—no matter how professionally trendy it was -- was begging for trouble for a black woman in the corporate world. I didn't mind dressing in suits so much though because the only thing that I took more seriously than my writing was how I looked. My mentor in college, who became my department chair once I returned as an instructor, cautioned me to remember,

> *"It is hard for women in leadership, my dear, and it is near impossible to be an attractive woman in leadership. You are a natural leader. You are extremely intelligent, excessively compassionate, and unfortunately for you, my dear, you are also very beautiful. Everything that you do will be scrutinized just because of your face that has the added misfortune of being attached to that shape. I say this not to scare you but rather to prepare you. You will be lied to and you will be lied on. Live boldly and walk heavy. If you are going to make a difference, make it in cement. If you are going to make a point, make it in stone. If you are going to make a mistake, make it your own. Own everything about you, but never let a jealous bitch make you hers."*

I miss that woman.

All of the professors had mini suites where their students could sit and wait for appointments. Each professor, I came to learn as I was being escorted to my mini suite, had a full-time assistant. For a small university, they definitely had big university benefits.

My suite was dark when we walked in. Dr. Abebaw handed me my keys and motioned for me to open the door to my new office. When I did, the lights came on and several people yelled, 'Welcome home!"

My tendency to become overstimulated in a short amount of time was not appreciative of the noise, but I was able to hide the discomfort from my face.

In a blur and a rush, a swarm of people approached me patting me on the back and half-hugging me. My head was swirling and my heart was beating so hard and fast that I was sure that it was visible through my shirt. I was just about to start the fainting sway and look for a way to escape when I heard a familiar voice behind me.

"Damn, let her breathe. She don't know yall's asses like that!"

I didn't need to turn around to know that it was my best friend, my spicy Filipino firecracker of a sister, Thuy. I might have mentioned that she was man crazy, but I probably should have just left it at the crazy part. We all had our roles in our friend group, Leah was the serious enforcer,

Thuy was the crazy interrogator, and I was the nerdy investigator.

"Thuy!" I exploded with a level of thankfulness that I couldn't even pretend to hide.

"Yep. Get ready for it." Thuy walked over to me and then hugged me because she knew that my feet were firmly cemented to the floor.

No one reacted to Thuy. It's Thuy so what exactly were they going to say? I am sure that they were used to her by now. She may seem harsh on the outside, but she is, by far, one of the nicest people that you could ever have on your side. However, that mouth of hers is lethal!

As people naturally formed groups and began eating the food that was laid out, I finally had an opportunity to look at the faces in the room. There were about thirty people walking around. I couldn't say that there was more of one thing than another: there were men and women, black, brown, yellow, white, and a few people that could be combinations of a few. Some appeared to be younger than me, but most of them seemed to be my age or older. All of the variants and tropes of English professors were present, as well: the trendy dresser, the sassy older one, the one who looked like an English professor, the one who probably smokes weed in his office, the one who probably burns sage in his office, the one who still dresses as if the sixties were last year, and an array of people from different countries who represented well through their clothes.

Once there was a quiet hum in the room, Dr. Abebaw signaled for everyone's attention.

"Good morning. I would like to take this opportunity to celebrate each of you for being here and taking the responsibility to welcome Dr. Hawkins home. You will find that she is the missing piece to our puzzle."

With an embarrassing amount of enthusiasm, my head popped up when he mentioned puzzles. Did I tell him about my obsession with puzzles? Surely I did not. I wondered if he knew what kind of puzzles that I liked? Did he do research on me? Is it weird that I like puzzles so much? I wonder if he likes puzzles, too, I will have to ask him. Maybe I will buy him a—

"Hawk!" Thuy was whispering my name through clenched teeth, "stop thinking about them damn puzzles and say something."

I gathered what was left of myself, straightened my jacket, and mentally found an appropriate mask.

"Thank you Dr. Abebaw for all those kind words. You left me a little speechless for a moment. I am looking forward to working with each of you and I am also looking forward to growing together as I am sure that we all bring a wealth of knowledge and experience to the table. I am humbled by all that you have done here and I promise you that I will do all in my power to become a positive addition to the falc—family. My door is always open—-except when it is closed."

My new colleagues laughed and began to file out of the room, still grouped up in various pairs and threesomes. Just as the room was just about clear, I noticed a heavy-set woman with tight sponge roller set curls and what appeared to be a permanent scowl painted across her face in the corner staring at me. When she noticed that I was looking at her, she began walking towards me, but before she could get to where Thuy and I were standing, Dr. Abebaw stepped in front of her.

"Dr. Thomas. I wanted to speak to you for a moment, if you do not mind?"

The woman forced a smile and then looked in my direction once again as if to silently protest, but once she realized that Dr. Abebaw was not offering options, she resigned.

"Of course Dr. Abebaw. My office?" She suggested.

"Yes." He smiled at her, motioned for her to exit in

front of him and then when Dr. Thomas was standing in the hall, he turned to me and Thuy. "Dr. Hawkins."

"Yes?"

"There is nothing wrong with being as you are. As a matter of fact, it is you that the world has been waiting to see," He smiled, "Enjoy your day and do not stay in this office too long."

When I was sure that he was completely out of earshot, I closed the door. Thuy laughed.

"Shit's creepy, ain't it?"

I laughed. "No, it's not. It's nice to be seen."

"Well hell, I *see* you. How can I *miss* you with that fat as—"

"Girl, shut up." We both laughed. "Ok, so tell me everything that you know about Dr. Thomas."

"Hmmmmm. Let me see. Well. She is a whole bitch. She is a half bitch. Oh yeah, and she is a quarter-stealing hating ass bitch. Watch ya back."

"You don't like her?" I replied sarcastically and fake innocence.

"Don't nobody like her snaky ass. She is the reason why we can't keep the English department full. I actually think that she is a witch."

"Ohhhh, so you were actually trying to say *witch* earlier."

"Now you know damn good and well that I meant everyone of those bitches. Don't be looking at me like that. Everybody ain't super saved."

"So *I* am super saved now?"

"Oh hellllll no! I'm talking about Mom and Dad. Hey, did Mom send you with food? Because I miss it!" Thuy had the pleasure of eating like a linebacker and never gaining a pound.

"No, she did not."

"Then what have you been eating?"

"I do know how to cook, Thuy."

"No ya' don't. Well, not like Mom. Plus, I know that *you* do not have anything to cook in."

"What makes you think that?"

"'Cause you triflin'." She said as she added more chicken wings to her already stacked plate.

"Why are you like this?"

"You love me. Now, I asked you what have you been eating? Do you need food? Oh, and give me my key."

No matter where we have lived, we have always had keys to each other's places. Thuy and I got really close after Leah left school. She became like the sister that I had always wanted. My parents loved her like she was my twin. She stayed in as much trouble as I did and my parents had no problem disciplining us both. Thuy's mother was a widow and owned two businesses that kept her busy and away, so she was very glad that my parents unofficially adopted Thuy. They were both family. Right before we graduated, Thuy's mother even joined my parents' church.

"I had dinner at a restaurant that is in my neighborhood." I said while avoiding her glare.

"By yourself?"

I hesitated, "Yes," knowing that technically I was not lying.

She looked at me. I hate when she looks at me. I do not think that there is one person on this earth that knows me better than Thuy.

"Bullshit."

"How can you be so pretty and your mouth be so ugly."

"What's his name?"

"Who?" I protested. She gave me the death stare. "Azim." She won.

"Where did you meet him? What does he look like? And what kind of name is Azim?"

Before I could answer all of the questions that she shot in my direction, there was a small knock on my door.

"Come in."

A short, young woman stepped in with a tablet.

"Hello, Dr. Hawkins. I am Ashlee Jacobs—your assistant."

I motioned for her to come in and extended my hand to her.

"Nice to meet you Ashlee. You weren't at the reception?"

"No, I am taking a class this semester and I was trying to get enrolled before you got here. It took longer than I expected. I—-I told Dr. Abebaw."

"No worries. Education always comes first. Did you get everything figured out?"

"Well kinda, but I will go back during my lunch."

"Nonsense. I have nothing for you to do right now. Go back and get that taken care of and we can get acquainted tomorrow."

"Are you sure? I really want to work here. I worked in human resources last semester and that place is super busy. Definitely more work than study."

I nodded. "I am sure and I can't imagine that I will be so busy that you won't have time to study, too." The worried look on Ashlee's face disappeared and was replaced by a huge smile. Just as she was about to turn around and leave, I felt as though I had seen her before.

"Do I know you from somewhere?"

"I don't think so. I just have that kind of face. People are always confusing me with someone else."

"Maybe. Well, I will see you tomorrow, Ashlee."

Almost before Ashlee could close the door, Thuy was back asking questions.

"Answers."

I told her how I met Azim and how he cooked for me and walked me to the grocery store and bought my food.

"After a freakin' day? I have been here for years and you walked into Texas just snatchin' up good men! Does he have a brother?"

"Girl, I don't know. I just met him."

"Well, *met* him some more and ask some damn questions."

I laughed. I am so glad that I decided to move here and be close to my sister. There is absolutely no other place that I would rather be while I mend this broken heart than here with her crazy self. I looked at my sister and debated on whether or not I should tell her about my date tonight. When she caught me staring at her, I decided that I had nothing to lose. Besides, she knew me so well that she probably could already see it in my eyes.

"He asked me to come back to dinner tonight."

"What time are we eating? I'm just playing. I have to work on some stuff tonight, but don't forget to—nevermind, hand me your phone."

I handed her my phone and she made sure that our locations were still being shared with each other.

"You know Momma says that we ain't never too grown to let somebody know where we are." She reminded me.

"I know, I know. It should still be sharing my location." I looked over her shoulder as she checked the app. "Come help me get this stuff out of the car."

"Where did you park?"

"Not too far. It is by Dr. Abebaw's office."

"On the other side of the campus? Chile, I wish I would be seen tracking some boxes across campus looking like this." She pointed to her tailored suit and red bottom pumps. "I know that you are all 'I can do it by myself' but sometimes you don't have to, sissy. You have to start letting people do what they do so that you can do what you do."

"I know."

"What, no protest? Geesh, he really did a job on you last night, huh?"

"We're not talking about that here."

"Ok, ok, ok. As long as you know that if I had been there I probably would have caught my first body."

"Your *first* body, sissy?"

"The first one that you would have known about."

We both laughed. My sister was indeed what the dictionary would have labeled a 'ride or die.' That is why I had to be careful about what I told her. She wasn't the type of person that would kill someone, but she would definitely help get rid of the body.

The campus was becoming more lively and students were finally filing out of the early classes and interacting. If there was one thing that I loved about working on a college campus, it was the proximity to all things expressive. Being around people who were still trying to find out who they were and what they liked and what their purpose was, grounded me. As much as it was difficult for me to make daily decisions about my own life, I became someone different when it came to teaching. Well, I don't become a different person, I am just really confident in my ability to get people to see and understand things.

When I was in college, no one could have told me that I would have ended up as a college professor, but now that I am one, I can't fathom what else that I would be doing— other than writing and that does not have to happen in a vacuum.

As we passed by students, they all seemed to know and to love my sister. I wish I had had someone like her for a professor. She's funny, but no nonsense. She would laugh with you as you tell her that you stayed out too late drinking and are now babying a hangover, but she also wants that paper done and turned in on time.

Before we got to the parking lot where my car was parked, Thuy stopped walking.

"I need to pop in here for a second."

She went into a small white building. It was not as elaborate as the other buildings and if Thuy had not gone inside, I might have missed that it was actually a building. For most of my life, I have prided myself on my overactive observational skills but since I arrived in Bedford, I was becoming a little angry with how many details were escaping me.

While Thuy was in the building, I took the time to really look around. The campus was so beautiful. It was not a large school, by any means, but the landscapers used their skills to create the illusion of rolling hills and valleys. As far as the eye could see, there were places dedicated to providing shade and warmth and places for students to just hang out. It felt like a town. l was getting lost in the wind's song and the funny way that it was causing my hair to play with my ear, when I turned around to see if Thuy had come back.

"Took you lon——-" I couldn't finish my sentence because it wasn't Thuy that was standing in front of me. It was the same man that I had talked to when I was going to the convenience store last night. Although seeing him was a bit of a shock, I was not vain enough to think that he was following me; he didn't give me those kind of vibes.

"You would be amazed at the things that the wind knows, professor."

I briefly contemplated what he said and then decided not to directly respond to it.

"Are you a student here?"

"I used to be. Now, I have the privilege of being a student everywhere."

"I bet that is going much better for you than going to cold classes everyday."

He held his head to the side and looked at me for the briefest of moments. The angle of his head allowed the sun to seep into his eyes until they harnessed the sun just enough to sparkle. His long thick eyelashes and mocha brown eyes evoked just a hint of jealousy from me. He smiled like he knew that I was lost in thought about his eyes. I had not noticed his smile the first time that we met; his beard (that was now gone) must have hid it and those dimples.

"Funny. Out here, no grades, but the marks you get and the classes that you take determine when you graduate."

"Not one lie in that."

Again he stopped, gazed at me deeply, smiled, and then lowered his head. He backed up nodding to some truth being spoken to his mind and only he could hear.

"Nice to see you, again, professor."

I smiled. I cannot explain it, but I felt connected to him. He lived such an uncomplicated life and being around him made my mind rest. He spoke in a paradoxical language that was like a mind puzzle and it calmed me.

Not breaking his backward stride, he placed a hand to his heart and nodded. It was a slight nod, but a nod it was and then he was gone.

"That man makes my willies grow legs and walk." Dr. Bisson said. She was staring in the direction of the man with whom I had been speaking.

"Oh, why is that?"

"He's like a cat, just everywhere and you never know he is there. He has popped up from one too many corners for my liking."

"I can see how that would be unsettling. You don't think that he is dangerous, do you?"

"You know," she walked closer to me and placed her hand on my arm. As she leaned in, I could tell that whatever she was going to say, she did not want other people to hear.

"I could have sworn he was following me home the other night. I had decided to go on a walk to get to know my little neighborhood and although I didn't see him, I definitely felt like someone was following me."

"But you didn't see *him*?"

"I can't be certain, but the way that he is always everywhere but also nowhere is just suspicious on its own, don't you think? The university needs to do something about having random strangers milling about. We must keep our students safe."

Before I could offer my opinion, Thuy came out of the building and joined us.

"Dr. Bisson. I see that you have met my sister."

"Your sister?" She shifted her eyes from me to Thuy and then back again. "Why isn't that just lovely! I would suppose that knowing the right people will always be the best advantage to opening doors."

Thuy's soft look turned into one that is normally what I would call a Leah. look coupled with a mimic of Dr. Bisson's heavy Southern drawl.

"And whatever do you mean by that?" Thuy mocked Dr. Bisson's exaggerated southern speech.

"Oh I meant nothing negative by it. I am sure that your family helped Dr. Hawkins rise from some horrible circumstances. I am more than acquainted with the hard stories like that." She reached out to pat my hand. Her eyes met mine as if she was waiting on me to corroborate the assumption that she had made about me and my family.

I gave her none.

When she could get no response from either of us, she brightened her eyes and found her wrist.

"Lord, if it ain't already time for me to get to this next meeting! It was so nice seeing you both again."

We mirrored her polite and fake smile and followed her with our eyes until she was out of earshot.

"That bitch is crazy."

"Thuy! Your mouth is always on ten. What if she had heard you?"

"What? You were thinking it and I said it. See, that's ya problem. You be so worried that you are going to offend '*tha Lord*' that you keep all that shit bottled up on the inside. Well, I hate to break it to you little sister–"

"Little sister?" I interrupted.

"Ok, shorter sister, anywho. God knows what you are thinking anyway. Momma always says–and it is probably in the Bible—but since I have *not* read it, I'm just going to say that Momma said it—-it is not what goes in that messes up people, but what comes out and she was not talking about cussin'."

"You know you are always teasing me about being super saved, but you are the one that is quoting scriptures all day. Maybe *you* should be a minister." I said half-jokingly.

"And maybe you should shut the hell up before I call both of our mothers and tell them that you haven't been here but a day and you are already making booty calls."

"Why are you like this?" I paused after each word.

We both laughed. As we headed to my car, I noticed that there were some men with a truck parked behind it.

"Looks like we will have to wait for a little while."

"Naw, they are meeting us. Girl, you are so used to having to do everything for and by yourself. Not me. I love you but if you thought that I was going to help you lug all that shit up to your office, you definitely do not know me like you think that you do."

I opened the trunk and the car and the gentlemen retrieved the boxes for me. I felt horrible that I had packed so many books to put in my office, but I have to have them. I always have books around me: books in my work office, books in my home office, books in my purse, and books on my phone. If you see me without a book, there is definitely a problem.

When they were finished, we got into my car and drove to my side of the campus so that I could park closer to my office. Before we reached the parking lot, I saw that man again.

"Hey sissy. Do you know anything about him?"

"Him who?"

I pointed to her side of the car, "That man over there."

"Oh you talking about Kamar. Kamar Prosper. He fine, huh?"

"Get help."

"No, he *is* fine—got that quiet-starving-artist-poet-painter-serial-killer, vibe."

I laughed, "Serial killer? And *that* is sexy to you?"

"Don't judge me."

"Oh, I am definitely judging you." I quickly responded. "I don't get the serial killer vibe from him. We actually have had a few interesting conversations."

"Conversations? Word around here is that he doesn't talk—to anyone. You being the serial killer whisper was not on my bingo card."

"Really, Thuy?"

"See, that is the problem. When a person is not going around blabbin' all of the time, people get to make up what they don't know and since he ain't talkin' there isn't really anything to separate the fact from the fiction."

"I don't know," I shrugged my shoulders, "I like him. There is something about him that is so relaxing."

"I can see that for you. You know, with your autism and him being low-key and untethered, he probably is relaxing for you. Of course, I am sure that it helps that he is the finest homeless, serial killer that I have ever seen."

"Please stop." I laughed.

"Now that I really think about it. That pepper and salt beard is giving daddy. And you can just tell that them abs is all vegan, no sugar, no carbs, and raw. I bet he can eat–"

I quickly interrupted and looked around hoping that no one had accidently heard her. I knew that she was about to go off the rails and there would be no coming back. "Stooooooooop!"

It was times like these when I both hated that Thuy was my friend and loved that she was my sister. She was a pro at keeping me in stitches and on the train straight to hell.

"You know I'm just playing. Well, kinda. If you don't want him, slide him my number. I might be down with a little choking."

I picked up the phone and called my mother.

"Hey my sweet baby. How is everything going?"

"Thuy is out of control." I giggled as I snitched in between words.

Mom let out an exhausted sigh, "Put her on the phone."

I pressed the speaker so that I could get the satisfaction of hearing Thuy get into trouble.

"Heeeeey mommy." Thuy said innocently as she stared daggers into my soul.

"What are you doing to your sister?"

"Doing?" She looked like she couldn't think of what she could say. Then she stared deeper at me and smiled the most diabolical smile that she could. "I'm not doing anything. I was just telling Bella that she should be cautious about spending so much time with this man that she just met on the street."

I tried to turn off the speaker, but Thuy grabbed the phone before I could.

"Wait, what man? Bella?" Mom yelled.

"Mom, you know Thuy is not to be trusted." I screamed as I chased Thuy around the room.

"Uhmm, hmmm. She is not the only one." Mom laughed. "Y'all get off my phone. Love you both."

Thuy threw the phone on the couch and fell out laughing.

"You know I am going to kick your ass for that, right?"

"Ooooo, wait a minute, Bella used a cuss word?" She lost control laughing. Then she jumped up and kissed me on the cheek. "Well my work here is done."

"You are so messy. Why didn't you tell Mom about Azim instead of Kamar?"

She stopped walking and turned around and looked me in my eyes, "Because he is the only one that you talked about without me asking. Bye sissy."

Chapter Seven

While I was unpacking and setting up my office, I changed my mind several times about whether or not I was going to go back to the restaurant to see Azim. Having someone show some concern about me and my needs was nice, but not only do I not trust men, I do not trust myself with men. The purpose of being here was to start over, and I do not want to find myself back into the same kind of foolishness that I was in. I don't want to be the one taking care of everything anymore. I do not want to be the one who is always giving encouragement or the one that has to always figure everything out. I want to be held. I want to have a shoulder to cry on. I want someone to curl up under on cold nights and watch movies or just to listen to the crackling of the fireplace. I want to be surprised with trips and gifts. I want someone who can take my serious business side and not conflate that with my goofy side–because I do have one. I just have never had someone in my life that I felt comfortable enough to let all of my sides out. I want to want someone desperately and I want someone to want me—completely.

When I think about the love that my parents had, I wonder if that is just not possible now. I am in no way a 1950s type of girl and there is no way that I am staying at home cooking and cleaning and waiting on my man to come home, but I wouldn't mind working *together*. I don't expect perfection; however, I cannot and will not ever be comfortable with a man who lies. If you can lie about who you are at your core, then you are capable of anything. I don't mind the work, I just don't want to do the work and think that I am building something with someone just to find out eleven years later, that he was only pretending.

That's the hard part. Being autistic means that I sometimes have difficulty understanding people's intentions when it comes to personal relationships. When I was younger, it was *excruciatingly* difficult. I would stay at friend's houses too long. I knew that they were ready for me to leave, but I would forget *how* to do it. I would have all of these thoughts running through my mind and my body would become heavy with thoughts of what could go wrong if I got up. Honestly, I didn't even like most of the people that I was around. I especially didn't like how they made fun of people once those people would leave.

Even though I could not decide if going to the restaurant was a good idea or not, I did notice that when I

got home, I showered and took more care with my
appearance than I normally would.

The weather was very mild, so I wanted to enjoy the
walk over. Just like before, I saw Kamar standing near the
light like he had been waiting for me.

"Hello, you." I smiled and didn't shy away from
walking close to him.

"Kamar."

"Excuse me?"

"My name."

I nodded and responded, "Bella."

He smiled, tilted his head forward and said, "I know."

When I didn't give him a negative reaction, his tense
shoulders seemed to relax.

"You mind if I walk with you?" He said in a low voice
that was slightly above a whisper.

"I would actually like that."

After I said that, he turned and extended his hand
like an usher would if he was directing me to my seat. Once I
started walking, he instinctively matched my stride. Having
short legs either meant that I had to walk faster than
everyone else or that I was going to get lost in the crowd so
it was inviting to have someone who matched my steps
perfectly.

"I know." He joked.

I smiled. I knew that he was talking about how we were walking and not that I wanted him to walk with me.

"I won't see you at the school anymore." He said with no emotion.

"Why?"

"Dr. Bisson."

"She didn't get you banned from the campus, did she? She had no right to—"

He interrupted, "No, she didn't. I would rather see you here."

"Here?" I wondered if the only time that I was going to see him was going to be at the stop light.

"Where the wind blows."

This might have been the first time that I had been thankful that my level of melanin was so high because I was blushing like a teenager. Neither of us said anything else. We just walked and listened to the wind blow through the trees.

Right before we reached the restaurant's door, Kamar stopped walking.

"You don't want to come in?"

"I think Azim would consider that just a little bit crowded."

"Where are you going?"

"I like walking. I will walk around until I want to go home."

"Home?"

He laughed out loud and again I was caught off guard by his dimples that sat like parenthesis on each side of his perfect smile. "I'm not homeless, Dr. Hawkins. I definitely have a place where I sleep and eat." He laughed. "It even has a bed in it."

"I didn't mean to insinuate that you were homeless."

"Most people think that I am."

"Does that bother you?"

"That reveals more about them than it does me."

"I guess that I am no better than they are."

"And that makes you the best of them."

"How?"

"Even though you thought that I was homeless you looked beyond my circumstances and just saw a man." He looked around and hung his head down, "I will see you soon, Dr. Hawkins."

"Bella."

He stopped walking and looked in my direction for just a brief moment. He didn't look at me; he only whispered, "Bella."

He turned and walked towards the convenience store on the corner. It wasn't until I turned my head towards the restaurant that I actually remembered why I was there. I opened the door and walked in. I didn't know what I was going to say if Azim wasn't there or was not around to greet me. Since it was only the second time that I had been there, I couldn't walk in and expect for people to remember me or for me to have an established table.

Azim was standing at the door. The sight of him almost took my breath away. I did not remember him being this fine. I laughed a little at his attempt to dress up. The dark suit and tie did not look natural on him, but it did look good. He was smiling and wasted no time walking over to me. Before he spoke, he inserted his arm under mine and guided me to the other side of the restaurant. I had hoped to sit in the same area as before, but I didn't want to expose all of my issues so early in the—in the what? This was not a relationship. At best, it was a date and a date meant nothing.

"I wasn't sure if you were going to come or not." He admitted.

"I appreciate you for inviting me," There were about fifteen other responses that I had to weigh through my social mask. I didn't want to seem too eager. I didn't want to sound too unimpressed. I didn't want to divulge too much of my personal information and I definitely did not want to make some weird noise like the one that was twirling around in my head.

I promise that I do have a personality. Well, kind of. I have created a personality of borrowed characteristics that I like about people that I admire. Sometimes I am Claire Huxtable. Sometimes I am Analise Keating. Sometimes I am Sinclair from Living Single pretending to be Sandra from 227, but that always comes across like Aunt Esther from Sanford and Son. God forbid if I ever dared to let out of my mouth what was actually in my head.

"You have a standing reservation here every night, if you wish." He said.

"That is very kind of you. I am sure that the owner would have something different to say about that though."

"I am sure that he would agree with me." He winked at me.

It took longer than it should have for me to realize that he owned the restaurant. That is the thing about my bestie Autizzy, she never works when you want her to. Sure I can detect patterns and small details about butterfly activity that never escapes me, but something that actually means something is lost to me.

"Well," I attempted to flirt, "tell him that I will have to figure out a way to thank him for his kindness." I immediately regretted that. That sounded like I was giving up tail feather for a meal and I was not. That is what happens when Rose pretends to be Blanche.

"Not needed. Just showing up is the repayment. Besides, I am really enjoying researching and perfecting the gluten-free recipes. Because of you, I will be adding them and vegan options to the menu."

"Really? That is amazing! It is so difficult for people like me to enjoy eating out." I beamed way too much.

"I also am trying to find some alternatives to dairy and looking into adding a little variety to my tea selections. Recently, I had a customer scold me for not having sweet tea."

Before I could laugh at knowing that it had to have been Dr. Bisson, I heard some women laughing from the bar. It was the same young ladies from the night before. When Azim noticed that I was looking at them, he got a puzzled look on his face.

"Do you know them?"

"I don't really know anyone yet. I remember them from last night"

As the women fell into each other completely engaged in laughter that involved tears and brief breaks before even louder bursts erupted, the shorter one looked in our direction and bolted from her seat dragging the other one along.

"Dr. Hawkins, I thought that was you!" Ashlee sang.

Ok, so let me tell you a little bit more about my girl Autizzy. Until I have *other* reasons to know a person, I tend not to know them outside of the place where I met them. Now, this is not a rule and it can absolutely change at any time. "Ashlee, how are you?"

"I'm great. Just hanging out with my bestie, Emilia." They seemed to glow like Infinity stones the closer that they were to each other. It made me think about my college days with Leah and Thuy. I wondered if we used to look like that.

"Emilia, do you go to the university, too?"

"I do. I am an English major."

"An English major? I wasn't sure that they made any of those any more. I thought that we were a dying breed."

"Oh no! I love all things words. Like literally, all things words."

"Tell her about your award winning blog and your podcast!"

Embarrassed, Emilia whispered, "I have an award winning blog and podcast."

"Ugh! No, *tell* her about it."

As if for the first time and thankful that she would have a valid excuse, Emilia looked at me and then she looked at Azim.

"Clearly, she is busy right now." She said with an expression that I could not place. Was that frustration or embarrassment?

"I would really like to hear about your work. Maybe you can stop by my office tomorrow and we can chat a little bit more?"

"I would love that." Emilia said.

"Come by anytime. My calendar is pretty clear for the rest of the week."

The girls walked back to their seats at the bar and continued laughing and talking.

"Dr. Hawkins? What do you teach?" Azim asked.

"I'm an English Professor."

"An English professor? So you will be grading me during our conversations, right?"

"Yes." I joked.

"Well, how am I doing so far?"

"I will let you know." I finally flirted successfully! Thanks Sandra.

He laughed and said, "I'll be back in a sec," and tapped the table as he got up.

When he returned, he was holding a plate that looked strangely similar to the one from the night before. He sat the plate in front of me and returned to his seat.

"Are you going to just sit there and watch me eat?"

"I love watching you eat. Your eyes dance and your shoulders sway a bit like you are listening to some good music."

"Did you just call me fat?" I laughed.

"Did I?" He laughed, faking innocence.

"If you keep feeding me like this, I will be."

"Nothing wrong with a little weight. It just means that you are happy."

"I am not ready to be that happy, yet."

"So you would like me less if I put on some pounds?" He stood up and pushed out his stomach and cheeks. "I'm still sexy, right?"

"Still?"

"Ohhhhhh!" He grabbed his heart like he was having a heart attack and fell back into his seat. "You cut me deep, girl!"

"You'll survive." I smiled.

"Eat your food." He got up and walked away towards the kitchen.

My phone rang. I didn't have to even look at it to know that it was Thuy. My sister was the queen of perfect timing.

"Hello?" I sang.

"Singing? You must be eating. Where is our new boo?"

"He went to the kitchen and he is not my boo."

"Boo, bae, bitch, Same difference."

"What do you want my dear sister?"

"I never want anything but to fill your life with flowers and bullshit."

"And you have, you most definitely have."

"Call me when you get home, goofy."

"I will."

"Was that your safety call?" Azim said as he slid back into the booth.

"My safety call?"

"You know, the call that your friend makes to give you a way out of a date that is not going well."

"What? I would never." I laughed. "I would just get up and leave after I told you that I was not liking it."

"You would do that?" Azim said with a shocked look on his face.

"I would." I assured.

"I like that. That tells me that you are honest."

"Honesty is the most important thing to me."

"Then we will be just fine."

"We?"

I have to admit, even though I was in no way ready to be in any kind of relationship with anyone, Azim was the kind of man that I would want. He is stable. He is protective, caring, funny, and attentive. I just hope he is willing to take this as slow as a sloth crawling into a molehill.

I sound like Dr. Bisson. Autizzy strikes again.

Chapter Eight

"Good morning, Crissy."

"Good morning, Dr. Hawkins. You look amazing."

"Thank you. Do you know if there is anything that I should add to my calendar?"

"I gave Ashlee a copy of the department and main campus calendar. I believe that she is working on it right now."

"Thank you for doing that."

I have to admit that I was impressed that Ashlee was already at work and taking initiative. If there is one thing that I have learned in my professional career, it is that a good assistant is hard to find and even harder to keep.

I had not even approached the door to my suite before I smelled my favorite coffee brewing.

"Is that my praline lavender latte?" I asked as I floated towards my door.

"It is. I didn't know what time you would be in, but I figured that it would be early. You don't mind that I started it for you, do you?"

"I absolutely do not mind and if my hands were not full, I would hug you very tightly."

"Let me get the door for you." Ashlee hurried around her desk and opened up my office door.

"You are an angel. Give me about five minutes then come in so we can get acquainted."

There was no way that I was going to be settled in only five minutes, but I could at least catch my breath and drink some coffee. Truth be told, I don't know how long it was going to take for me to feel comfortable in this new place. I hated *having to* move even more than moving; I equally hate having to start over. In the right circumstances, there could be something very refreshing about having the opportunity to begin again, but it was just as plausible that I would tote all of my fears with me into a new space which blocks all of my old hopes.

I kept remembering what Dr. Abebaw told me yesterday. If I was honest, I was not sure that I knew how to "be myself," but at this big age and late stage in life, who else was left for me to be? Being like everyone else was tiring and being alone was—well, lonely. I enjoy my private time, but more and more, I was waking up from dreams in which I was not alone anymore only to be disappointed.

Ashlee came into my office five minutes later with her tablet, notebook, and pen in hand.

"Are you ready for me?"

"Yes. Can you lock the outer door so that we won't be disturbed? We can leave my door open."

"Of course."

She locked the door and then returned to the office and sat down in the chair that was in front of my desk.

"Let's go to the table by the window. Would you like a cup of coffee?"

"Actually," she said cautiously, "I would."

"Please help yourself. You are always welcome to have coffee or snacks or whatever food that I have in here."

I remembered being in college and although I didn't have extreme money issues, it was tight because I did my best to live on my own and not have to rely on my parents for more than tuition. They would have supported me fully with no problem, but I knew that it wasn't easy running a church and a business.

"I didn't expect to see you last night." She said, breaking the silence.

"I think we saw each other the other night, too." I said finally identifying that she and Emilia were the two young women that walked in with me the first night.

"We did?"

"Maybe not. So do you and Emilia go there often?"

"Practically every night. It's down the street from our gym and not too far from Emilia's mom's grocery store."

"The one on the corner? Is her mother, TiTi O?"

"Yes, that is her mother."

"Well this town is getting smaller by the day. I met her mother a couple of days ago as well."

"That's Bedford for you. I have only been here for a year and that was the first thing that I noticed."

"Just a year? Aren't you and Ashlee related?"

"Why do you ask?"

"You two look so much alike. I thought that you had to be sisters."

"Well you know what they say, the longer that you hang around someone, the more that you begin to look like them."

"Perhaps." I took a sip of my coffee. "So where is home for you?"

"I'm originally from Louisiana."

"I would have never guessed that."

"Why, because you don't hear the accent? I do my best to keep it down, but if I get super comfortable, it comes out."

"I love the Louisiana drawl. You are the second person that I have met from Louisiana this week."

When I said that, Ashlee frowned, it wasn't long, and she attempted to cover it up, but it was definitely a frown.

"Oh really? Here on the campus?"

"Actually, yes. Dr. Bisson. She is new, too. I first met her at Emilia's mother's store. She was raving about their sweet tea."

"I haven't heard about her. What does she teach?"

"I believe that she said that she was in the psychology department. I don't know much about her. Dr. Abebaw introduced us briefly."

"Louisiana is a big state." Ashlee looked out of the window and quietly sipped her coffee.

"It is indeed. So what are you majoring in?"

That question seemed to further disturb her. She didn't react negatively, but it was the way that she was very intentional in her responses that led me to believe that she was struggling with making that decision.

"Coincidentally, I am a psychology major."

"Oh?"

As if she was understanding my curiosity about her reactions, she attempted to explain. "That is why I was so confused about not knowing who Dr. Bisson was."

"That makes sense. So are you in your Junior or Senior year?"

"I wish. I am actually just starting out. I took some classes at a community college at home and decided to transfer to a university for my major courses."

"That is very smart and I am sure that it was cost effective."

Her phone vibrated. She tried to hide it and slid it under her thigh.

"This is just us getting to know each other. Please check your phone. I think that I will find mine, too."

Being in college is never easy and starting later can make it unnecessarily challenging. I was glad that Ashlee seemed to have found a friend that would help her along the way.

When I got to my desk, I had messages from Azim, Thuy, my mother, and from my father. I expected all of them except the one from Azim. I knew that he liked me, but that has always been a weird experience for me. I have a hard time telling if someone is being sincere with their intentions towards me which is exactly opposite when it comes to seeing the malintentions of others towards the people that I care about. I have a hard time regulating my emotions and trust is something that has become a struggle for me. This is not the same, or at least I do not think that it is the same, as someone who has been in horrible relationships one after the other and has now developed a cynical view of all men. Because I have lived the majority of my life masked, I have difficulty accepting that people like me—like the real me. I am constantly wondering if they are attracted to the me that they think that they see and over time, that me becomes more difficult to maintain because that is but a small percentage of the total person. I am sure that everyone struggles with some form of this, so I don't know if I am that different or if this is, yet again, something that only happens to people like me. My mind is constantly trying to solve the autistic puzzle so that I can just insert the final piece that will leave me as normal.

I looked up from my phone to see if Ashlee was waiting on me. She was feverishly texting, so I decided to respond to a few of my messages to pass the time.

To Azim: Good morning.

To Mom: Hey mommy!

To Dad: Good morning Daddy!

To Thuy: Why are you harassing me this early in the morning?

I didn't have long to wait before my phone was flooded with responses.

From Azim: Will I see you tonight?

From Mom: Are you getting settled in?

From Dad: What classes are you teaching?

From Thuy: Bite me bitch. Meet me for lunch.

To Azim: Not tonight, I really need to get settled in.

To Mom: A little. I think I am going to make Thuy help.

To Dad: I am so excited, I get to teach Women in Literature!

To Thuy: Want to help me pick out some stuff for my apartment?

From Azim: Need help? I am great at building things and I could cook for you.

From Mom: Tell her that I said that she needs to help you.

From Dad: That is right up your alley. I wish I could sit in and get a few pointers.

From Thuy: I think we should go back home, and get all of your stuff out of that asshole's house.

To Azim: I appreciate the offer. Raincheck?

To Mom: She is trying to convince me to do a drive-by on Marcus.

To Dad: Said the greatest preacher and teacher this side of heaven.

To Thuy: I told Mom on you.

From Azim: I am going to hold you to that.

From Mom: My babies keep my prayer life very active. Do NOT and I repeat DO NOT do a drive-by with your sister. (smiley face)

From Dad: What is your mother talking about? Who is doing a drive-by?

From Thuy: Snitch bitch. Meet me at the salad bar around 11. Love ya.

To Azim: Please do. TTYL

To Mom: Really??

To Dad: Nobody is doing a drive-by. I will call you later. Love you.

To Thuy: You are unhinged. See you at 11.

Ashlee and I finished our text conversations about the same time so I moved back over to the table.

"Do you remember my friend Emilia? She really wants to talk to you about her projects. Can she come in?"

"Of course she can. I would love to hear more."

Ashlee shot up from her seat and was at the door almost before I said yes. When Emilia came in, she was just as nervous as she was last night. I wasn't quite sure if it was because I was one of her professors or because she was not as excited about sharing about her projects as her friend was about telling me about them.

"I am so glad that you decided to come by this morning, Emilia." Although she was holding her head down slightly, I noticed that she took a quick questioning glance at her friend. "Tell me about everything that you have going on!"

"Well," she said shakily, "I've always wanted to be a writer. When I was in high school, I wrote some poems and my English teacher entered one of them into a contest. I didn't know that she was doing it. I wasn't mad. She probably knew that I would not have done it on my own. Well, it won and it was published. That is when I started to believe that I might actually be good at it and then I started a blog and a podcast."

"That is quite an accomplishment. You should be proud. Some writers don't ever get national exposure." I wanted her to know that she should be proud.

Beaming with so much pride that you would have thought that she had written the poem, Ashlee interjected, "She was on the news everywhere!"

That made Emilia's smile fade slightly as she gave Ashlee another confused look. "So many people came to Bedford to interview me. Most of the time they would come to the school, but one reporter showed up to my mother's store." It was easy to see that there was more to that part of the story. "My mother was furious at my teacher."

"Furious?" I questioned.

"My mom is not big on attention. I can't tell you when the last time was when she took a picture. I wasn't even allowed to be on social media until I was in college."

"In these days and times, I can fully understand that. The internet can be a scary place for a parent. I am sure that your mother and father only wanted to keep you safe."

"It's just me and my mom. My father died before I was born. He and my mother had broken up and before they could figure it all out, he was killed in a car accident."

"Oh, I am so sorry. Well that definitely explains your mother's desire to keep you safe. She had already lost someone that she loved."

Ashlee made a small sound. I wasn't quite sure if she was trying to add on to the conversation or if she was responding to what had been said.

"What about you Ashlee? Why did you decide to major in Psychology?"

"That is easy. I wanted to know why people do what they do. You know? Like why do good people do horrific things." Briefly she looked towards the window. It was as if she was lost in thought and had forgotten that we were in the room with her. "When I was a kid, I would hear about messed up things that people would do. Like getting behind the wheel after having a lot to drink. The person hits someone. That person dies. Tragic, right? But no one really thinks about how that one decision continues to form the reality of the people who were not even there."

"That is so true." I really contemplated the depth of what she had said. "One decision can change everything for everybody."

"See, that's why we," pointing to her friend Emilia, "make so much sense." Emilia seemed to come alive while Ashlee was talking. "I want to know the *why* and Emmy wants to tell the story and sometimes finding out the story behind the decision can reveal the why."

"I don't think people realize how important understanding human behavior is for writers. To create emotionally and structurally sound characters, you have to know their whys and tell their stories in a way that hides as it unfolds."

They both looked at me as if seeing me for the first time. I had not even noticed that they were both sitting on the couch.

"Well, if you want the rest of that lecture, you will have to enroll in my course."

"Wow, that makes me want to take the class, too." Ashlee said.

Emilia pulled out her class schedule and pointed. "I'll be there in the front row!"

"I look forward to seeing how your writing grows this semester. Ladies, I have enjoyed this way more than I should have, but I better do some work or you may have to teach tomorrow."

They laughed, gathered their things, and headed towards the door.

"Do you want me to close the door, Dr. Hawkins?"

"Yes, thank you."

I decided to work at the table next to the window. Before I got started, I saw Dr. Abebaw walking across the yard and it reminded me of what he told me:

"There is nothing wrong with being as you are. As matter of fact, it is you that the world is waiting to see."

Chapter Nine

I do not remember when the last time I *had* to have an alarm clock wake me up. Don't get me wrong, I will always set my alarm, but I will never use it. I don't sleep long enough to use it. Every morning, without fail, when I look at my phone, it is 4:44 a.m.. Even though I awoke at the same time this morning, I didn't get out of the bed like I normally would. I laid there trying to calm my nerves.

The first day of school is the portal to my anxiety. I worry about what to wear, how to enter the classroom, and how to introduce myself. What never supplies me with angst is what I will say. Once I am done with the preliminaries, another me kicks in. I love teaching. I think that I got that from my father. He was a pastor well before I was born. I've been to many churches (it kinda comes with the territory) but there is nobody that does it quite like my dad. He doesn't hoop and he doesn't holler; he teaches–then he hoops and hollers. He doesn't build his sermons based on the emotions that they evoke, he connects. I don't know how he does it, but I have been told by my students that that is what they love the most about me. They feel connected to the subject, to the lesson, but most of all they feel connected to me. I wholeheartedly believe that students can learn from anybody and they will learn whether you want to teach or not. However, it has been my experience that students retain information and apply skills more if they believe that the person who is presenting the information believes that he or she is important. My dad does that too, but somehow, when he does it, you don't feel more connected to him, but rather to God. I never start a new semester without praying for guidance, innovation, and strength. Teaching is not easy and truth be told, I have thought about quitting every year since I started.

Earlier in my career, I taught in public school. If you ever want to know anything, teach children because they tell everybody's business. Because I have this need to help everyone within two feet of me, I struggled with discerning which stories were true and which were concocted to garner a response and some sympathy from me. Being a mandated reporter also meant that regardless of whether or not I personally believed the story, there were some things that I had to act on. Over the years, I have seen just about everything and even with that being the case, when children are involved, I could never become jaded.

However, you also shouldn't become so involved in your work that you cease to live outside of it. I saw that happen to a few teachers along the way. They would be so convinced that the student was telling them the whole truth that they failed to see how much of their responses were being controlled by their own traumas. It never ended well. That's the challenge: care enough to be sensitive and aware but not so much that you fail to see clearly and become easy to manipulate.

Now that my brain was fully awake and crawling out of the random rabbit research hole, I decided not to spend too much time trying to find the perfect outfit for work. I made myself breakfast, read my devotional, and then read over my notes for class one more time. By the time that I was ready to go, all of the nervousness had left my body and had been replaced with excitement. I ran downstairs and out of the backdoor and there was Kamar waiting by my car.

"How did I know that I would see you this morning?" I said while greeting him with a smile.

He didn't respond. He only extended his hand to offer me a brown bag. It was heavier than I expected it to be.

"What is this?"

He looked down at the bag signalling that I should just open it. I unlocked the passenger side door and placed my laptop and purse inside. Then I opened the bag that he gave me. It was a glass orb. It wasn't large and probably could have fit in my hand, but it was heavy. When I turned it, I could see flickers of colors that sparkled slightly depending on how the light hit it.

"It's beautiful. Did you make it?" He nodded, looking up but not raising his head fully. "For me?"

"Everything is something. People spend years trying to excavate the same truth that had already been uncovered. It just wasn't accepted. Ain't nothing new; it's just revealed."

"So—," I vocally thought through what he was saying, "it is a waste of time trying to fit in because you can only fake it for so long before who you really are will bust out."

"Exactly."

"I needed that confirmation this morning. Thank you for stopping by and thank you for this beautiful reminder." I walked around to the driver's side of the car and got in. Before I drove off, I rolled down the window to ask him to come by later, but he was gone.

When I pulled into my space at work, Thuy was standing there like I was in trouble or something.

"Only an hour early? I have never seen you be late for anything."

"Didn't you just say that I was an hour early?"

"Early for the rest of the world, late for you. Where you been Penny?" She was referencing a famous line from one of our favorite childhood television shows, Good Times.

"Why are you here?"

"I wanted to walk you to class, you know, let everybody know that you are *mine*."

I laughed. "I can't believe that people allow you to teach."

"You know you love me."

"With my whole heart I do. I also think that you should be evaluated."

When I walked into the lecture hall, I was shocked by how many students were enrolled. When you are teaching an elective class that only English majors are typically interested in, you do not expect large numbers. I wondered if each section was going to be as full as this one. Perhaps all of the English majors were in this class, I thought.

"Good morning everyone," I made a point to look directly at as many students as I could. "While I am getting logged into the screen, please scan the attendance code. Once we get started, if you have a question or would like to respond to something during class, say your name first so that I can put names with faces." What they didn't know was that before the end of the month, I would know the names of all of my students.

"Please be sure to do your attendance before the end of class. The code changes every day and closes five minutes before you leave." Shuffling and rearranging let me know that they had not initially done what was asked.

"I thought so." I whispered to myself. I gave them a few more seconds and then began. "Hopefully you are in the right room. This is Women in Literature. This semester, we are going to delve into the world of writing from the female perspective and how customs, race, ethnicity, ideologies, geography, culture, and laws influence how we perceive stories about women, for women, and from women. And, before you ask," I interpreted the tightness on the male students' faces, "there is a class about Men in Literature; it's called World Literature." A few of the female students laughed and looked at each other while a few of the male students blushed.

"Each semester," I continued, "I choose a theme that we will use as a lens to frame our conversations about the stories we read. This lens is not the only lens that can be extracted from the literature; however, it is the lens that we will be using. Feel free to offer additional perspectives in your writing, but do your best to step outside of the familiar and endeavor to explore what is not, necessarily, commonplace."

Before I could continue, a hand in the middle section caught my attention. That was the first time that I noticed that Emilia was in the room. "What is the rationale for us looking at the literature from one perspective when we all bring life experiences that add value to what we read and connect us to what we read?"

"That is a great question. You are 1000% correct. We all have experiences that add to our ability to connect to the literature to deepen our personal understanding; our challenge; this semester is to focus on one experience and endeavor to find a way to see it from a point of view that is different from our own."

Emilia nodded that she finally understood. A young man in the back of the classroom raised his hand.

"So, basically, you are telling us what to think?" A few of the students laughed as if to signify that he had made a point of contention; therefore, exposing what he perceived to be my bias.

I laughed. "No, I am inviting you *to* think." The *oooos and ahhhhs* that quietly swirled around the room were very reminiscent of what it was like teaching fourth graders. "If you do not remember anything that I say this whole semester, I urge you to contemplate this: the only thing that is real is your perception of reality. As thinking individuals, we must always be willing to challenge our own perceptions by venturing to go where no one in our families have gone. To eat foods that your family has never tried. To travel to places that you have only heard about and to hold conversations with people who do not look like you so that your perception of the world can have a chance of being within the reach of being accurate."

The heaviness of silence in the room let me know that I had them right where I wanted them. "Find someone in the room right now. You don't have to get up. Just look around the room and find someone that you could easily identify as your opposite." Instantly, they did as asked. "Now right down all of the reasons that you chose that person as your opposite." I gave them a few minutes to write. "Most of you chose race and gender first, then physical characteristics: I'm-tall-she-is-short kind of stuff. Maybe you looked at hair length and color. Perhaps you looked at their clothes. A few of you may have been able to even use religious differences."

Feeling slighted and determined to garner the admiration of the class, the same male student from before said, "Cory. My name is Cory. We chose those things because that is all we could choose. Now, if you had said to interview a few people then we could find out other stuff."

"Thank you Cory. You are right. I could have asked you to interview all of the students and then to find a person that was your true opposite. That would have taken some time, but we could have done it. Even still, your choice was going to be based on the information that was presented." I looked around the room. "How many of you would have thought to ask if the other person had been bullied? Not likely, right? Why? Most of us would not have asked that question because it would have revealed something about us to the other person that we did not want anyone to know."

I walked closer to the area where Cory and his friends were sitting. "I am not trying to trick you. I only want you to consider that your perception of reality is limited; therefore, it cannot be true; it can only be real."

Cory looked at me and slowly spoke like he was learning the words as they came to him, "In order for us to find out what is true, we must be willing to accept that our reality is limited based on our experiences."

I smiled, turned, and walked back to the front of the room and whispered to myself, "Got him."

I changed the slide to share about the final project. "We are going to deep dive into some very common pieces of literature— many you have probably read in high school. The goal is not to get you to read but rather to think. In your syllabus, you will find the list of stories that we will discuss this semester. When you read them, I want you to focus on the duality of human nature. I want you to consider how good people do bad things and how good people do bad things for good reasons. I also want you to ponder how good and bad lies within each of us and what experiences and circumstances determine which side of us prevails."

Chapter Ten

Being back on a college campus was really good for me. I could tell that I was starting to feel like my old self. The only thing that I hated was that the air conditioner had superpowers. I decided to leave my office and take a walk around the campus. It was late, but I wanted to do some research for this novel that I kept telling myself that I was going to write. My short stories and poems had gotten positive reviews and had even won some awards, but for some reason I had been able to just sit down and begin. I hadn't found anything that inspired me, but being here in Bedford, was starting to get my creative juices flowing.

The challenge for all writers is not to become so engulfed in writing that you forget to walk. I could stay in research and typing for weeks, so I loved the fact that I had a safe place to walk around. I decided to see more of the university and visit some areas that I had not been able to during the day. The Humanities building where my office was was closer inside the campus. I assume that was because it was a building that all of the students would need at some point of their matriculation. The more specialized buildings were tucked off further down the hill with winding trails that faded into nowhere. Once you followed them, it was like finding a hidden valley. The trees were tall but not towering and the tops were just forgiving enough that you could easily watch the sun set. It was breathtaking and made me just a little sad that I did not know how to paint. Instead, I decided to take a panoramic picture of the view, capturing as much of the scene as I could. As I turned around slowly in a circle, I felt like a little kid.

"You look free." I didn't feel the need to concoct a story to explain what I was doing and I didn't need to try and figure out who was standing behind me.

"I feel free." I turned around to look at Kamar. "What frees you?"

"Painting. Mixing colors. Listening to the music of the colors. I can hear the songs."

"Synesthesia."

"Now it is but when we were kids, it was just weird."

"I know. My parents had to fight to get the doctors to diagnose me. They seemed to be comfortable with me being a genius but autistic was just going too far."

"My parents were not so vigilant. I was an only child in an adult world that was so complex that what some call superpowers now only considered them to be points of contention and disgust then."

"They didn't understand?" I asked.

"They didn't see." He explained.

"Maybe they couldn't see." I protested.

"They didn't see because that would explain too much and not everybody wants to know themselves. We have a world full of people that spend countless hours trying to fit in and be normal. Not so that others can accept them but–"

"So that they can accept themselves." I interrupted.

He smiled. "Don't get me wrong. I don't know how I feel about me, but I do know that I am the only me that the world is going to get so I might as well do the work."

"I admire that about you, Kamar. Don't get me wrong, my parents were amazing, but they still only see what they perceive to be who I am."

"Which is?"

"Like my father." I looked at him and found such peace in his eyes, "He is a pastor, actually." I waited for his response.

"I can see why they believe that. You have a way of leading people to truth that is very unique. You make people want to be. Maybe they're right, but in the wrong way. My parents saw me, they just didn't like what they saw because it was so different from the path that they chose for me."

I took a moment to consider what he was saying. Was I like his parents? Was I running from who I was because I didn't like the path?

"No." He answered my thoughts. "You don't like it because you don't want that same gift to manifest in the way that it did for them. But think about what you do everyday. You educate. You challenge. You lead people to truth—and that is church."

"Hey, do you have a minute? I want to show you something."

He bowed and motioned for me to lead the way. When we arrived at my building, I took him to my office. I opened the door and turned on the light.

"What do you think?"

He walked around and looked at every inch of the space.

"It's nice but it does not feel like you."

"Is that what it is? I like the space and I love the window, but I don't love it, you know?

"You like colors so why don't you have any in here?"

"I am starting to think that you know me better than I do."

"Nah, I just see you."

"It's nice to be seen."

He smiled so big that it was almost cartoonish. "Ok, Dr. Hawkins, it is time for you to go home. Unless you have a dinner appointment, this evening." There was something in his tone that I had not heard before. Was that jealousy?

"I do not have plans for dinner, but I should be getting home. I didn't realize how late it was. It's the weekend, what is there to do around here?"

"Around here? I can assure you that there is always something to do in Bedford. That is why I love it here. It's very artist friendly."

"Good to know. Maybe I will see you around this weekend?"

"Probably not. I have a project that I am working on and I want to finish it."

"Oh." Why was I so disappointed? He was just a friend and I was acting like a love-sick teenager that was told that her crush had a girlfriend.

The weekend went by without much fanfare. I spent time with my sister and we finally bought cookware for my apartment. I don't know why I had been avoiding doing so. I guess it felt like I was starting over again and I didn't want to get comfortable. When I was younger, buying new things was exciting, but now it felt like failure. I wanted roots. I wanted a backyard. I wanted an address that was just mine. I wanted a garage. I wanted lazy Saturday mornings draped in my bathrobe and fuzzy house slippers. I wanted romantic evenings lying on the couch wrapped in the arms of my forever. I wanted to be awakened by morning breath kisses and comforted by arms that would never leave. Buying dishes, in yet another apartment, felt like I was giving up hope of having a home.

I made fun of Thuy about being man crazy, but was I any different? Maybe she wasn't man crazy, maybe she just was relentless. Neither of us had reduced life to being meaningless without a man, but we both knew that what Mom and Dad had was something to be desired. Truth be told, we were more alike than I would like to admit.

When I got to my car Monday morning, I expected to see Kamar standing by it. I don't know why, but it seemed like that was going to be a thing for us. I placed my bags in the car on the passenger side, no Kamar. I walked slowly to the driver's side, no Kamar. I got in and put the car in reverse making sure to look behind me and still no Kamar.

I stopped by the corner store. I had been wanting to try the coffee shop since I found out that there was one and repeatedly forgot to do so. I parked my car and went inside.

"Good morning." I said to TiTi O.

"Good morning. I remember you. You came in with Azim."

"Yes, I did and I have been thinking about this place ever since." I looked at the menu on the easel on the counter. "Which do you suggest?"

A familiar voice came from behind me, "They are all great."

I turned and smiled at Emilia. "I totally forgot that Ashlee said that this was your mother."

"Ma this is the professor that I was telling you about." She beamed.

"She has not talked about anything else but that first class."

"Oh, how sweet."

"She said that you were a badass."

I laughed. "I don't think anyone has ever called me that."

"Well you are. Cory and his friends are stupid. You wouldn't even guess that they are actually upperclassmen. It's like they do that kind of stuff to every female professor. It's the whole 'females are dumb until I need them to do my work for me' bull."

"Maybe this class will help change everybody's mind." Had she been a little older, I would have told her that people only behave like that because of their own insecurities, but it wasn't the time or the space. Her mother handed me my cup and I handed her my card. "I will see you later. Make sure that you have finished all of the readings."

"All of them?"

I gave her my teacher stare.

"I'm just kidding. I read them this weekend."

I smiled at her and her mother and then I left.

It was still early enough that I normally would not have had to tussle with traffic near the university, but this morning was quite a bit different. I wanted to be nosey and see what the congestion on campus was all about, but the road had been blocked off, so I drove directly to my office building.

When I walked in, coffee and bags in hand, I was met with groups of the professors crying.

"What happened?"

Crissy walked over to me. I am sure that she was the only one that had even heard or seen me.

"Dr. Bisson was found in her office—dead."

"What? How horrible! I didn't even know that she was sick."

"I don't think that she was sick."

"Then what happened?"

"I'm not quite sure, but the police have been asking people questions. My friend that works in that building said that they have Dr. Bisson's office blocked off like a crime scene."

"A crime scene?" I said a lot louder than I had intended. I moved closer to Crissy and whispered "they think that she was murdered?"

"It seems like it."

"Oh my dear Lord. That poor woman. Why would anybody want to murder her?"

"You did *meet* her, right? Her face was full of confusion.

Understanding Crissy's implied meaning, I responded, "I know that she was not the nicest person, but was that enough to cause someone to—you know?"

Crissy shrugged and walked back to her desk. I walked to my office still in a daze. I was surprised to see that Ashlee had beat me to work.

"I wasn't expecting to see you this early, Ashlee."

"I had a class first thing this morning, so I came in right after to make your coffee."

"You are so sweet. Did you hear what happened?"

Ashlee looked towards the window. "When I was walking to the building, I saw the police cars. I didn't want to get too close."

"That makes sense. Oh, remember that professor that I was telling you about? The one from Louisiana? They found her in her office."

"She had been there all weekend?" Ashlee asked.

"I'm not sure. It's so very sad."

I opened the door to my office and immediately noticed a beautiful painting hanging behind my couch. I didn't need to ask who had done it, but I was curious as to when he had done it. When I turned around, Ashlee was standing in the door and grinning.

"Delivery guy brought it in. It was so beautiful that I asked if he could hang it up. I hope that that was ok."

My eyes watered as I looked at the painting. It was a woman standing in the middle of a prism of bright colors while standing barefoot on the beach. You could only see her back, but I knew that it was me and I knew that Kamar had painted it just for me.

"It's beautiful." I whispered.

"You know, the longer that I look at it, the more that I think that woman looks just like you. No wonder you bought it." She smiled. "Well, I am going to head on to class."

I nodded and walked over to my desk. I looked at my phone for the first time that morning. I had texts from Azim and Thuy:

From Thuy: Girl, did you hear about Dr. Bisson?
From Azim: Good morning. Can I see you tonight?

To Thuy: Girl yes! I'm sorta creeped out. I heard that they think that she was murdered. I wonder why?"
To Azim: It may be late when I get off.

From Thuy: What the fuck? I mean she was a bitch but damn. I'm coming over there. They cancelled all classes today, anyway.
From Azim: I don't mind. I miss seeing you. I'll wait.

To Thuy: I wonder how Dr. Abebaw is doing.
To Azim: I can drop by at about seven-ish.

From Thuy: Ok See you in a few.
From Azim: I can't wait.

I opened the door to my office to see if Ashlee had left yet and a man in a police uniform was standing there. "May I help you?"

"Are you Annabella Hawkins?"

"I am. And you are?"

"I am Sheriff Justin Bailey." He showed me his badge. "I am here investigating the incident that happened on campus."

"Oh yes. Of course. Please come in. I'm sorry, my nerves are just a little shattered."

"My condolences. Were you and the decedent close?"

"The decedent—Dr. Bisson? No, I wouldn't say that we were close. Both of us were new to the university."

"You weren't friends?"

"Not exactly. I've only seen her a few times. We were always cordial. We had talked about having lunch, but we never got around to it, unfortunately."

The Sheriff took a few notes and then he looked around the office. "And your name?"

Thuy had walked in while the Sheriff was asking me questions. I gave her the hardest stare that I could to try to get her not to say something foul.

"I am Dr. Bautista, assistant Dean of the Math department."

"My condolences to you as well. Did you know the dece–" he looked at me, "Dr. Bisson?"

"As my colleague communicated, Dr. Bisson was a new member of our university family and since we were in two different buildings we had very little interaction with one another."

I wanted to look to make sure that it was Thuy that was talking. It looked like her, but it had been a long time since I had heard something that wasn't laden with cuss words and freaky tales come out of her mouth.

"Dr. Hawkins, where were you Friday evening at approximately seven pm.?"

His question caught me off guard and I did not have time to put on my professional mask. "I don't know."

"You don't know if you worked late Friday?" He said skeptically.

"No, that is not what I mean. I mean that I am not sure where I was at seven, but I did stay on the campus later than I normally do. I do remember that the sun was going down."

"Why were you here so late?" He asked.

"I had not completely set up my office so I worked on that for a while and then I took a walk around the campus to get familiar with the locations of the building."

"At night?" He asked skeptically.

"The campus is beautiful and I wasn't ready to go home, so I decided to take a walk—to wind down, I guess."

"Where did you go?"

"I think I pretty much walked around the whole campus at some point." I said while I was trying to retrace my steps in my head.

"Do you remember going by the Psychology building?"

I took my time to think about my answer. I turned to Thuy and asked her before I answered. "Is that the building that is downhill? She nodded.

"Yes, I did! It was so peaceful and I could see the sun setting just beyond the treetops." Sheriff Bailey smiled and as if he caught himself, and then stopped abruptly.

"Do you remember what time that was?"

"I'm sorry, I don't."

"Did you notice anything strange?"

"I had never been back there, so I wouldn't know if anything was out of place."

"What did you do after that?"

"I went home." I paused for a moment. "No, I went back to my office. I ran into a friend and I quickly showed him my office. He walked me to my car and then I went home."

"What is your friend's name?" The sheriff's eyes widened.

"Kamar Prosper."

The sheriff stopped writing and looked at me with one eyebrow lifted.

"Boyfriend?"

"Friend."

"Do you know how I can get in touch with Mr. Prosper?"

"Unfortunately, I do not." My response piqued the Sheriff's curiosity.

"But he is a friend." He said as more of a point to ponder than as a question. He looked from me to Thuy, "You both have been extremely helpful this evening. Here is my card, if you think of anything else or if you need anything, please feel free to call me."

"Thank you." I took the card. "Sheriff, can I ask a question?"

"Sure. I might not have the answer but go for it."

"Was she murdered?"

Shocked by my question in a way that I didn't think that he should have been, he asked, "Why do you ask?"

"I think this whole thing creeps me out. If she died–unassisted, then I get it, but if someone—ummm," he nodded that he understood, "then I need to rethink my working schedule."

Chapter Eleven

I might have paid a little more attention to my appearance than I had in the past as I got ready to see Azim. I grabbed my keys and my phone and instead of walking over to the restaurant, I decided to drive. Once I got to the car, I rolled the window down and Kamar was standing there. For the first time, I felt startled.

"You're scared of me now?"

"No, of course not. I just was not expecting to see you."

"What's new about that?"

I turned the car off and got out basically to prove a point. He looked at me taking in my whole image and smiled, "Azim."

I really didn't want to discuss Azim with him. I am not sure why, but it just didn't seem right. I didn't want to lie to him so I didn't respond to the question that was hidden in his comment. "I love the painting." I paused for a second, "Is it me?"

He didn't answer. I was stuck looking at him. My head had been lowered slightly so I took my time to really take in his presence, his strength, and his weakness. What he wasn't saying made me a bit dizzy and I found it difficult to stand, so I rested my back on my car. He stepped closer to me than he had ever before. How had I not noticed how good he smelled? With each step, I forgot how to breathe but also breathed so deeply that I could have fainted. I wasn't sure what he was doing, but I had never wanted anybody to do it more than I wanted him to do it right then. I looked away. He took his hand and placed it gently on my cheek and raised my head until my eyes met his.

"Have fun." He moved his hand away and then walked away. I knew that if he walked away I was never going to see him like this again and I was also sure that I did not want that.

Before he disappeared, I called to him, "Kamar." He stopped walking and returned to the exact space where he had left me breathless. "Why were you on campus Friday?"

He closed his eyes slowly, backed up, and bit his lip slightly. I had never seen a man sexier than him at that moment. After I asked the question, I wanted to capture the words and throw them down the street, but I also wanted him to just answer me. I couldn't tell what I was seeing in his eyes–for the first time.

"When you realize that you know the answer to that already, I'll be here."

And with that, he walked away and didn't look back.

I sat in the car and contemplated texting Azim and telling him that I wasn't feeling well, but I had blown him off so many times that it seemed unfair. So I started the car and drove to the restaurant.

As I expected, Azim was at the door talking to customers and being his perfect self. He *was* perfect. He *was* fine. He was upfront about how he felt about me. He was uncomplicated. He was emotionally available.

Mid-sentence Azim walked away from the couple that he was talking to and walked over and grabbed my hand. "This is Bella."

I smiled at the couple and expected them to go to their table and we would escape to ours, but they didn't.

"Bella, this is my mother, Husna and this is my father, Abdelaziz."

I cannot tell you the level of absolute anger that filled my soul at that moment. Surely this was not his way of having me meet his parents. We weren't even dating. "Nice to meet you both. Azim, do you mind if I speak to you for just a moment."

Trying to read my eyes, he softly said, "Of Course. Mama, Abba, go ahead and sit." and then he led me back to his office. He had to clear walking and sitting space for us. There was plastic on the floors and the desk and table. In the corner, there were paint cans and brushes.

"I know, I know, I know. I am so sorry. I did not know that they were coming tonight. Is it weird? Of course it is weird. I can tell them that you don't feel well and when they are gone, I can bring your dinner to you." Both pleading and hoping filled his eyes.

"It's fine. I actually don't want to be alone right now."

"I am so horrible. I heard about what happened on campus today. The girls told me when they came in."

"Right." I nodded remembering that I had seen them sitting at the bar in their usual spot.

"Are you sure you are up to this?"

"I'm fine."

We left his office and he held my hand as we walked to the table and joined his parents. Surprisingly, the dinner went quite well. Azim's parents were funny and treated me like family and not like I was being interviewed to be their new daughter-in-law which took a lot of pressure off of me. I cannot lie, I still did not believe that Azim had no idea that his parents were coming. Even though they also said that they had just dropped by, I kept getting this feeling like he was not being completely truthful.

When I got home, I found the strength to peel out of my clothes and into sweatpants and a t-shirt. I was too emotionally drained to even take a shower. I crawled into my bed and looked out of the window. I reached for my phone to check my messages. As I assumed, there were several from Thuy. I didn't feel like texting, so I called her.

"Hey sis, what's up?" I said through a long exasperated breath.

"I'm going to get straight to the point."

I sat up in the bed knowing that whatever she was going to tell me was going to be serious. "Ooooook."

"I have two elevated unholy fingers for all of the old women in our church—our mothers included, who walked around and didn't tell us that Perimenopause is a bitch!"

I knew that she was being very serious, but I burst out laughing. "Girl, you scared the heck out of me."

"You should be scared. Listen, I came home and I guess I took a nap. I say that I guess, because I don't remember falling asleep. Wanna know how I woke up? Of course you do. I woke up because I pulled a fucking muscle in my leg taking it out from under the covers and then putting it back under there because the room was hot cold! What the fuck is hot cold? Why is that term now in my every fuckin' day language?"

There was no way I was going to be able to get through this conversation without laughing so she was just going to have to be mad at me.

"Today," she continued, "I was in my office and I kept smelling something foul. I got up looking around thinking maybe I had accidentally left some food in the trash. Looked in there—nothing. I looked in all of the corners and in the little refrigerator—nothing. At this point, I consider that I might just be going crazy. So I sat down thinking that I was losing my mind. I cannot describe the utter horror in realizing that it was my own *get-up* air! The sweat under my breasts smelled like bad decisions and childhood regrets. If I throw another bottle of deodorant away, I will check myself in somewhere with rubber white walls and with a couture white jacket that wraps around."

"Oh sissy." I said as I wiped the laughter tears from my eyes.

"I feel like I'm going crazy. I'm crying at commercials and shit. I don't cry, I'm a thug and I am crying at fucking commercials! And every day, I throw a new pair of panties away because *patty pee pee down there* ain't the kind of wet that she supposed to be."

Now that I had caught my breath, I could actually think, "Did you set an appointment with your gyno?"

"Yeah, I did. Went before I came home. She prescribed some hormones."

"They will help you to feel better."

"I ain't old enough for this bullshit. I can't be sexy talking about, '*excuse me while I remove my plastic panties.*'"

"Perimenopause is not going to stop you from doing anything."

"Yes it is. I don't know if I am sweating or pissing. What if I start crying at the wrong time and some knucklehead thinks that I have fallen in love?"

"First of all, stop messing with anybody that can be classified as a knucklehead."

"Well, I would if you would stop taking all the fine men in town. Bedford ain't that damn big and the pickins is hella slim."

"What are you talking about?"

"First there was some brother named Azim, then there was the fine ass serial-killer Kamar, and now the Sheriff."

"The Sheriff? Ok, now you're reaching."

"I guess you didn't see how he was looking at you, huh?"

"Yes, I did. He was looking at me like I might have murdered someone or at the very least, knew who did." That was the first time that I had allowed myself to think about Dr. Bisson. We both got quiet.

"I wonder if she had any children." Thuy asked.

"That's a good question. I wonder if the university is going to send anything to the family. Maybe we can talk to Dr. Abebaw about it tomorrow." I suggested.

"We can put something together. I know that people didn't like her, but damn, she *was* a human, you know?"

We both got quiet again. "Do you really think that she was murdered? They are not acting like it was a medical issue or natural cause."

"I was wondering about that, too." Thuy said.

"Do you remember her first name? I'm going to see what I can find out about her on the internet." I put the phone on speaker and opened up the browser.

"Good idea. I think it is C-h-a-i-t-r-a."

"Yep, I found her. She was from New Orleans, right?" I took a few seconds to scroll through all of the information that came up. "Wow, she *was* very accomplished in her field.

Half of the page is filled with awards and recognitions on her work with the neuropsychiatric community."

"See anything about her family?"

"Not yet. Hey, here is something interesting. Did you know that she used to work for Child Protective Services?"

"Really? I definitely did not see that coming. I thought she ate children."

"Shut up. Looks like that may have been her first job as a psychiatrist. According to this article, she provided support for families and children that were in threat of being separated. I wonder if I contacted the agency, would they tell me if she had any family."

"Maybe, but if that was her first job, how long ago was that? Might be better to check with Human Resources here, first. Surely they would have information about her next of kin."

"Would they give that out?"

"Under the circumstances, I don't see why they wouldn't."

"I'll see what I can find out tomorrow."

Thuy yawned, "Ok. Lunch?"

"Of course." Before I decided to turn in for the night, I thought that it would be a good idea to stretch. I walked past the window and I thought that I saw someone standing outside. I couldn't tell if it was a man or a woman. When I doubled back, whoever or whatever I saw was gone.

After my shower, I finally felt my brain winding down. I grabbed my remote and found my regular show that I used to fall asleep to— The Jeffersons. When I started drifting off to sleep, my phone buzzed.

From Azim: How are you feeling?

To Azim: I'm ok.

From Azim: You know, I have never taken you out on a real date.

To Azim: What do you consider a real date?

From Azim: Meet me at the restaurant at 7? We won't eat there, I promise.

To Azim: I love your food. Where are we going?

From Azim: A place that I think that you will like. Not too far.

To Azim: Can I meet you there instead? I have some errands to run.

He didn't respond right away. I wondered if he was offended that I didn't want to ride with him. I didn't really know him and I definitely did not feel comfortable doing so.

From Azim: Of course. I'll send you the address. Is 7 good for you?

To Azim: 7:30 might be better.

From Azim: It's a date.

He sent the address and I intended on searching to see what the business was, but I fell asleep before I could.

When I got to work the next morning, I expected the campus to have a sullen feeling, but instead it seemed like no one really cared that Dr. Bisson was gone. In fact, they seemed happier. Now, I could have just been overthinking things, but it really did seem like she was not a very liked person. This made me sad. I could tell that she may have not been the nicest person, but I wondered *why* she was like that. I decided to go to Dr. Abebaw's office before I got locked up in my own for the rest of the day. I knocked on his door because there was no one at the front desk.

"Come in."

I opened the door. Dr. Abebaw was sitting behind his desk looking through papers. When he looked up, he appeared to be genuinely shocked to see me.

"I am sorry to bother you. I just wanted to know what I could do to support any kind of memorial efforts for Dr. Bisson."

The confusion on his face matched my own. "Please sit down."

I did as invited. "I know that she was new to the campus, so maybe she had not had time to make a positive impact yet." The way that he was looking at me made me very uncomfortable. "Am I missing something? Maybe overstepping my role here?"

His face softened and he began to look like the Dr. Abebaw that I had become more accustomed to. "Please forgive me. I am deeply saddened that you are the only person that has inquired. I was looking through some of the information that was emailed to me by HR and there seems to be information missing."

"Missing? From Dr. Bisson's file?"

"Well, yes. I wanted to reach out to her family and when I asked for her file to be sent electronically, there were parts missing" he took a deep breath "or maybe she had not had time to complete them." He stared blankly in my direction but I am sure that he was not looking at me. "I wonder what the police have been able to find out."

I thought about all of the paperwork that had to be completed when you started a new position and I could completely believe that she had not gotten through all of it yet. Actually, this was making me think about if I had completed everything that I needed to do for my own file. I reached into my purse to get my phone so that I could make a note reminder and then I saw the business card from the Sheriff.

"I have Sheriff Bailey's card here. I am sure that he would know."

"Would you mind contacting him and then letting me know what you find out? It would be a great tragedy for us as a family not to send something to her family in Louisiana." He looked at his watch. "I apologize for cutting our time together short. I have a meeting that I must attend. Unfortunately, we have to figure out what to do with Dr. Bisson's classes and the students enrolled in them."

I gave Dr. Abebaw a smile of sympathy and understanding and left his office. Losing one person, whether people liked the person or not, could cause a multitude of issues that would eventually affect all of us. I was a little surprised that the same people that welcomed me were not extending that same level of thought to Dr.

Bisson. It made me wonder if there was more to this university than I had originally thought.

"I can't go down that rabbit hole, right now." I whispered to myself as I got into my car. I needed to call the Sheriff, but I wondered if that was a good idea. Sheriff Bailey definitely seemed like he thought that I might have something to do with whatever happened to Dr. Bisson and I wasn't sure if calling him would add to his suspicions. When I got to my building, I sat in my car for a moment before I decided to just do it.

I dialed the number and he picked up immediately, "Bailey."

"Sheriff Bailey, this is Bella Hawkins, from the university."

There was a long pause followed by a small release of air, "I didn't expect to hear from you."

"I didn't expect to have to contact you, but I was talking to the Vice President of the university and we would like to send something to Dr. Bisson's family. We don't think that she had had time to complete all of her new hire paperwork and no one knew her well enough to know where to begin."

Sounding a little confused and disappointed, he said, "I see. So, how can I help?"

I couldn't tell if I was bothering him or if he was still trying to figure out if I had something to do with Dr. Bisson's death. "Is there any way that you could find out who we can send our condolences to? You don't have to give the information to me, I can give you the Vice President's contact information and you can share it with him directly."

I heard rustling of papers and keystrokes in his background. "I wish that I could help you with that, but it doesn't look like we have been able to get that yet." He breathed heavily and whispered, "Very nice of you."

"I didn't really know her, but it only seems right that we do something to honor her life."

For the first time, he seemed interested in what I had said. "That's right, both of you were new to the university. I know you were setting up your office. New job?"

"New everything. I just moved here."

"From where?"

"Oklahoma."

"That explains it."

"I'm sorry, explains what?"

"I pride myself on having a good memory and I have been racking my brain trying to figure out how I knew you."

"Knew me—I mean, you know me? Are you from Oklahoma, too?"

"No, I am from Texas. Got my degree from Xavier in Criminal Justice and then when I graduated I went to Oklahoma and stayed there for quite some time after I finished the police academy."

"HBCU fam! I graduated from Langston University."

"Much respect. I've heard some good things about Langston. Did you pledge?"

"Do you even have to ask? What did you pledge?"

"Guess we are double fam."

"Oh six." He said.

"Oh eight." I responded and then we both laughed. The tension that had been between us subsided. "I'm confused, if you went to college in Louisiana, when did we meet?"

"Oh we met way after college. I was already on the force when we met. We met the first night that I was out in that district. That was the saddest thing I had ever seen and it kinda stuck with me."

When he said that, I didn't even need to think deeper, "Leah. You were the officer that brought her home."

"I was."

"That was a rough first night on the job."

"It was." We both sat in weighted silence. "How is Leah doing?"

"I wouldn't know. I tried reaching out to her after all of that, but she—"

"It wasn't you."

"Oh, I know. I just really miss my friend."

"What about your other," he paused, "friends?"

"Thuy? She is family. Leah, Thuy, and I went to school together. We balanced each other. It feels like part of us is missing."

"What about your *other* friend?"

"My other friend?"

"Mr. Prosper."

"Hmm." Now I wondered if this whole conversation was his way of relaxing me so that he could ask questions about Kamar. "I just met him; I don't know much about him other than we both like art and writing."

"I am going to be straightforward with you Bella, you might want to be careful about who you call your friend."

"Is there something that I need to know?"

"Were you aware that Dr. Bisson was complaining about him?"

Although I knew that she was, I wanted to see what Sheriff Bailey knew. "Complaining about him?"

"She had told several people that she felt like he was watching her. She had even told the campus security that she didn't want him on campus. And," he continued cautiously, "he was on campus the night that she was murdered."

A cold shiver gripped my spine, "She *was* murdered?" As much as I tried, the tremble of fear overtook my voice.

"Yes. We got the tox screen back this morning, so it is now officially a murder investigation."

"I'm so confused. Tox screen? She was poisoned? Are you sure?"

"I am pretty sure. Especially since I am looking at the report."

"Poisoned? That seems so far-fetched. Like, wouldn't a knife or a gun or even strangling be—"

"Better?" He laughed.

"Ok. I was going to say that, but that was not what I meant. Who poisons people?

"A killer."

Chapter Twelve

When I got off the phone with Sheriff Bailey, I had to gather my thoughts for a moment. Was he telling me that Kamar was a suspect? I mean, he was on campus that night, but that didn't have to mean that he did it. Besides, I am almost one hundred percent sure that he was there to see me, but how would he have known that I was going to be walking back in that area? Were our encounters really just happening or was he watching me, too? Why did I believe everything that he said to me, but I found it difficult to believe anything that Azim said? How did Azim get into this train that was going off the tracks?

I got out of my car and walked into the building. "Good morning Crissy."

"Good morning, Dr. Hawkins. I have been meaning to ask, how is Ashlee working out for you?"

"She has been great so far, but I have to be honest, I don't have much for her to do right now so I let her study."

"Really? As early as she gets in, I assumed that you had her working on a big project."

"No. She is probably using the space to study in peace and I am totally ok with that."

Holding up her own textbook, "I understand that. Have a good day, Dr. Hawkins."

"Thank you Crissy."

Before I could open my door, I could smell the coffee brewing. If I kept Ashlee forever for just this one thing, I would gladly pay her tuition. I opened the door and Ashlee was walking out of my office.

"Your coffee is ready for you."

"I appreciate that." I was about to walk into my office then a thought came to me, "Ashlee, did you end up having Dr. Bisson as a professor this semester?"

"Why?"

I was startled by her response. It must have shown on my face, because she softened her tone.

"I'm sorry. I think I am still creeped out about her being killed on campus."

"Yes, that was a shock for me as well.

"Who do they think did it?"

"I don't know. It's all really sad. Oh wait, you are from New Orleans, too, right?"

She looked at me with suspicion. "I don't understand what that has to do with anything. I didn't know her. Do you think that somebody is killing people from Louisiana?"

"Oh no, that is not what I was saying. I was wondering if you had family there that could do some digging for me." Ashlee's face tightened. "I want to send something to Dr. Bisson's family, but I didn't know her well enough to have had that type of conversation with her."

There was a light tap on the door and then Emilia walked in. "Good morning, Dr. Hawkins."

"Good morning, Emilia. Did you come to see me or Ashlee?"

"Well, I came to ask if Ashlee could do a favor for me." She asked nervously.

Confused, I asked, "How can I help you?"

"Would it be ok if Ashlee makes some copies for me? I have this article for a paper that I am writing and I have to give it back to my professor."

"Of course she can if she doesn't mind." Emilia handed Ashlee the papers and walked out of the room. "Would you like some coffee?"

"I would love some!"

We both went into my office. I poured her a cup of coffee and we sat down at the table by the window.

"I should probably move my desk over here. I love looking out of the window."

"It is a pretty view of the fountain."

I nodded in agreement, "Emilia, did you ever get a chance to talk to Dr. Bisson before she was–passed away?"

"Wasn't that so sad? No, unfortunately I didn't. She came into the grocery store a lot though. Seemed friendly enough, but I could tell that my mother didn't really care for her."

"Now that you mention it, I was there one night when Dr. Bisson was, too. She said that she knew your mother from somewhere."

"I think that she said that to everybody."

"Why do you think that?"

"Thursday evening, I was working in the coffee shop closing up and waiting on Ash. When she got there, she helped me shut down. We went to the grocery side and Dr. Bisson was talking to my mom. I think that she likes some brand of tea that we sell, so she was ordering it by the box. She stopped Ash, stared at her for a bit and said the same thing to her."

"Really? What did she say?"

"Something like '*Bedford sho'* has a way of making the world just one little ol' neighborhood, don't it? I done seen so many people from home'."

"Well, that's odd. That sounded more like she was sure that she knew Ashlee."

"I thought she was, but when we got outside, Ashlee said that she didn't know her."

"I've been to New Orleans before to get on a cruise and it is not small enough for everybody to know each other"

"That's what I've heard, but my mother says she has never been there. You know they say we all have twins out there somewhere."

"Maybe but Dr. Bisson would have been a hard one for anyone to mistake. She was pretty unique. I am sure that if your mother or Ashlee had met her, they would not have forgotten."

Ashlee returned with the copies and the two ladies went into the reception area. I closed my door and looked over my notes for class.

As I looked over my notes, I started thinking about Kamar. I really expected him to be waiting by my car this morning. I don't know why he would have been there; I all but told him that I thought he was a murderer.

"Girl, you are tripping, tripping." I said to myself as I tried to refocus. I knew *nothing* about this man. I had called him my friend, but we weren't even friends. I only knew his name because Thuy had told me. I didn't know where he lived, but somehow, he was always around. Sheriff Bailey seems to think that Kamar had something to do with Dr. Bisson's death. Sure, she could be difficult and she did seem to dislike Kamar, but was that worth killing her for? Why did she think that he was following her? I don't believe that he was, but what if someone was and she just assumed it was him? She was new to Bedford, so who else would have had a reason to want her dead? What if she moved to Bedford because someone from Louisiana was threatening her and that was the person who was following her?

As much as I was allowing this new puzzle to consume me, I had to focus and get to class.

Chapter Thirteen

"Good morning class."

A few students mumbled a reply. The couple of students that had been talking when I walked in, ended their conversations and turned their attention to the front of the room.

"Last week we discussed the duality of human nature. Over the weekend, you were supposed to have read several short stories so that we could begin unpacking those stories through that lens."

The expected low-pitched complaints swirled around the room, but surprisingly not as many as I had anticipated.

"Let's start with Kate Chopin's, *The Story of an Hour*. Would anyone like to begin our discussion?" I looked around the room and somehow did not notice that Cory was seated much closer to the front and had raised his hand.

"Doc." He said to get my attention. I turned my head slightly and smiled. I wasn't quite sure how this discussion was going to go with Cory starting it, but I had taught long enough to be prepared to reroute the train if he took it off the tracks.

"I'm sorry Cory, I didn't see you. Please begin."

He rumbled through a notebook, then he looked up at me. For just a moment, he was focused on me for a symbol of courage.

"The protagonist was in a good position socially: she was cared for and she had a supportive family and friend unit. Well, on the surface." He paused, but did not take his eyes away from mine. "I got to thinking about the society part. You know, some say that the world is unfair and that they are being oppressed. You know the history here in America. Well, I have always thought that people—*black* people—were intentionally being combative by hanging on to old stuff."

The air in the room became tense and thick with defense and anger. We already had a murder. The last thing that we needed was additional bad press. I was concerned that this kind of conversation could lead to an all out race war on the campus.

"That's an interesting point of view."

"I mean think about it. I know slavery was bad, but how bad could it be if we eventually had a Black president." He finally diverted his eyes from mine and spoke softer but with more confidence. "That was until I re-read the story. A thought came to me. I don't know why, but it did and I wondered if—like I replaced the husband with white people and the wife with black people."

The room was so quiet that it was like no one was breathing. He swallowed with an audible gulp then continued.

"Slavery was bad, right?" He didn't wait for a response. "I think *some* people tried to fix it by putting things in place to right the wrongs so that America could move on. Laws were passed. Laws were abolished. All of this tug-of-civil-war seemed good on the surface, but I still couldn't understand why Black people were still so mad all of the time. I was like, we *gave* them everything. What else did they want? I stared at that story for half a night, until I fell asleep. Then, when I woke up, I got it."

I waited for him to continue, but he just sat silently. "You got what, Cory?"

"Black people didn't ask for anybody to give them anything. We can't give rights that humans naturally should have had access to merely by existing. We were patting ourselves on the back and scratching our heads trying to figure out why yall was still mad. But y'all wasn't mad, y'all just wanted to be free."

"So how do we apply the 'duality of human nature' lens to that interpretation?"

He frowned as he considered my question and then with the biggest frown-grin that I have ever seen he said, "We want to develop a relationship, but our history sucks. Instead of issuing out things assuming that we know what the other person needs, we should just ask. Because when we do something that we think is right—even if it is for the right reason— can be wrong if it is not what the other person needs or wants."

"Good people with good intentions fueled by bad information and bad circumstances can cause absolute destruction." I added.

Someone in the back row said, "How do you trust the person who has burnt you so many times, but promises to change?"

It was clear that we were moving far away from the short story, but when a teacher sees the wheels turning, it is hard not to enjoy the ride.

Before I could respond, Emilia said, "Changed behavior. That's the only way. Saying I'm sorry acknowledges the wrong, but that means nothing if the person keeps doing the hurtful thing."

For just a moment, I thought that I saw a tear in her eye. I made a mental note to speak to her later to make sure that she was ok.

"Human behavior is complex. Life experiences lurk deep under bad attitudes, unhappy dispositions, and destructive habits."

A girl that was sitting on the floor charging her laptop said, "Like a cheater. Yeah the wife may stay and they may decide to work it out, but if he keeps moving like a cheater he just keeps breaking her heart. He doesn't see that she is not upset about the past, but rather about the new stuff."

"Duality of human nature teaches us that even though he cheats, he may also desire to be a good husband. Sometimes people do things that are in them because of the things that someone *planted* in them. That destructive behavior becomes a comfort. If he or she is cheating, he or she may be really insecure and the stimuli of new people absolves the responsibility of accountability that is attached to the commitment with the old person."

"Like crack." Someone yelled from the other side of the room. The seriousness that had apprehended the class dissolved into laughter.

"Like all addictions." I laughed. "The thing with addiction is that the initial interaction is usually only a way to escape the pressure of a place of insecurity, but the more that a person indulges, the less control that he or she has and the addiction becomes a malevolent god that requires control of everything: money, attention, desire, hope, and in the most extreme cases the surrender of his or her life. Continuing with the cheater example, then the wife is left with thinking that her husband is bad, but he may only be trying to silence his own screams."

"Or maybe," the same girl from before interjected, "he just a hoe." The girls in the class laughed.

"Y'all wouldn't know a good man if he walked up and slapped you." Cory pointed out.

"First of all, that wouldn't be a good man, that would be a dead man. Second of all, the good men are off somewhere with their boyfriends." One of the quieter girls jumped up from her seat in laughter.

"Damn, who hurt you?" Cory blurted out.

"Ain't nobody hurt me. I ain't never letting a dude that close."

"So how is a good man ever going to get a chance with you if you keep pushing him away?"

The girl laughed and then looked Cory directly in his eye and asked him, "Why? Are you feeling pressed?"

The quiet girl said, "Welp, that'll do it!"

He shook his head as if she had made his point for him and before the conversation could go any further, class was over.

While I was gathering my things, I thought about the discussion. If you would have asked me a few years ago, I would have told you that I definitely knew what a good man was. I would have given the easy examples of my father and my husband. Both had been great providers. However, that is where the semblance ended. When my mother looked at my father, it was like she was falling in love with him every time he walked into the room. My father was worse. I think he literally stopped breathing when she was around.

It was like that when Marcus and I first got married—or at least it looked like that. I would like to say that I was caught off guard, but that wouldn't be completely true. I think that there was a part of me that was aware that he had kept me from his heart even though I shared his home. As the years went by, we felt more like roommates than lovers and I had gotten to the point that I was willing to live the rest of my life in a piece of a marriage simply because it was easier. I kept holding my breath waiting for *my* forever and it never came.

When I finally left my parents' house after the incident, I didn't want to deal with life and was fortunate enough not to have to worry about finances. I wasn't suicidal, but I also didn't want to live. It wasn't because my marriage had failed, but more so because I was tired of waiting for life to work out for me. There was some unusual heaviness in my heart and I couldn't shake it. I checked into a hotel and just stayed there day and night crying.

I think that I would have stayed in that room for another week, if I had not had a doctor's appointment. For the first time in days, I took a shower, got dressed, and left the hotel.

October 16, 2019, Oklahoma City

"You look like hell." My doctor said as soon as she came into the room.

"Well, I should because that is where I have been."

A wave of compassion swept across her face and she patted me on the back. "You are going to talk while I draw this blood." Dr. Green had been my doctor since I was a teenager and was definitely like the cool aunt that you told all of your secrets to.

When I finished telling her that I was getting a divorce, she didn't press me about the 'why' and I was eternally grateful for that.

"You will be fine. You are a strong woman."

"That's the thing, I am *tired* of being strong. I don't want to be strong. I want to fall all the way apart, but if I do, what does that say about my faith?"

"Your faith? You talking about the Bible kind of faith? " I nodded. "Everybody but Jesus was messed up in that book."

I laughed just a little bit because it was so true.

"Being a believer or a person of faith does not mean that you are not going to fall apart. It simply means that there is someone that is fully capable of putting the pieces back together." She kissed me on the top of my head and walked out of the room.

I laid back on the bed and I suppose that I had fallen asleep because I was startled when she came back into the room.

"Honeydew, we need to talk."

The seriousness in her face scared me and my head began swirling with the possibilities of what she was going to tell me.

"Just say it."

She nodded her head. "You're pregnant."

Chapter Fourteen

"Hellllooooo." Thuy sang as she broke into my thoughts. "So you are ignoring me now?" I turned around to see the gum smacking slightly irate sister of mine.

"I'm sorry, sis. I was just lost in thought." I said hoping that she would not press me to share more information.

"No worries. Are you ready for your date tonight? What are you wearing and where are you going?"

Until she reminded me, I had completely forgotten that I had an actual date with Azim.

"I have no idea. I will find something in my closet."

"You don't seem to be too interested in this date."

"No, it's not that. I am actually excited to spend some time with Azim outside of the restaurant. I think Dr. Bisson's death has hit me hard, you know.?"

"No, I don't." She laughed. "I'm just kidding. I get it. Well, I don't get it because she was a horrible individual that you just met, but I get you so I know that you are dying to find out what happened to her."

"I think that it bothers me more that we haven't found a way to contact her family. Like, it is possible that she will have died and the people that loved her, won't even know about it."

"I'm not being funny, but if there are people out there that loved her like that, then surely someone will come around to find out why they haven't heard from her."

Thuy made a good point. Maybe I was seeing a problem where there was none.

"You're right——-I know, I know." I resigned.

"Of Course I am. I was built right."

"Don't forget to mention humble." I laughed.

"Humble is for saints, I'm 100% *that* bitch."

"There is something seriously wrong with you."

"I know, but my therapist says that I am processing my feelings about my childhood or whatever the hell she said, so I am covered."

I looked at Thuy. "You're in therapy?"

"Don't be looking at me like that. I got shit, too."

For the briefest of moments, the air between us became heavy with thoughts and uncomfortable. I considered the times when we had not kept up with each other as much as we should have. I also realized that it was easy to be so focused on your own pain that you forget that life was happening to everybody.

"You want to talk about it?"

"Hell nah. I be damned if my shit end up in this novel that you *aren't* writing."

"Well dang, tell me how you really feel." I laughed.

"I always do."

After we went to lunch, I went to my office to finish some paperwork and to see if I could find out more information about Dr. Bisson. I just refused to believe that no one in the world would want to know that she was gone.

When I opened the door, Emilia and Ashlee were having an intense conversation.

"Is everything ok?" I said as I looked from one girl to the other.

Ashlee looked at Emilia as if she was asking for permission to share the details. Emilia only put her head down.

"I completely understand. Just know that if either one of you ever needs to talk, my door is always open."

Emilia smiled and I got the impression that she wanted to talk, but not now. I went into my office and opened up my laptop. I knew that if I was to ever have peace again, I was going to have to figure out a way to find Dr. Bisson's family. I was even prepared to fly to New Orleans if I needed to.

I searched the number to CPS and called to see if there was any way that I could get some information from them about Dr. Bisson. Unfortunately, the people that had been working there during the time that she was there, were all gone as were most of the files. The only thing that I was sure of was that she had been working there during the time shortly before and after Hurricane Katrina hit the area. There was so much utter devastation and destruction that it left holes in thousands of stories. As I perused the different articles, there were countless stories of missing children, inmates, and people in general. I wondered if that was why there seemed to be so little about Dr. Bisson. Maybe she lost her family during the hurricane. Could that have been the reason that she seemed so disconnected?

I had been in my office for hours before I noticed that it was way past five and getting closer to the time that I was supposed to meet Azim. Since we were doing more than just eating dinner, I rationalized that I would not have time to continue my research, so I left it on my desk, grabbed my purse and headed out.

I wish that I had given more thought to what I was going to wear on our date. It was our first real date and I was finally getting a little nervous. When I moved to Bedford, I had no intention of meeting anyone; I just wanted to reconnect with my sister and to find a place within myself where I could be at peace.

As I stood in front of the closet, I realized that I didn't have dating clothes. Actually, I didn't even know what dating clothes were. It had been such a long time since I had to care about that kind of stuff and at this age, I was more concerned with comfort and warmth than trying to be sexy.

Sexy. Now that was a word that drove me completely batty mostly because I don't even know what that means. Thuy was always pointing out to me who she considered sexy but if she was conflating attraction with sexy then I would be forever lost.

Sexy, to me, is rainy days cuddled in the corner of a couch watching some movie—preferably one with a lot of fighting and explosions—while laying my head on his lap as he strokes my hair. Sexy to me is laughing so loud that I snort and cry while he looks at me like he won the lottery. Sexy is him accepting me and all of my weirdness and letting me completely unmask. Sexy is having someone who values me so much that he would never intentionally do anything that would jeopardize our home or our happiness. Sexy is him knowing that of all of the things that I want from him so that I can feel safe, secure, and loved is everything that I will be for him as well. To that man, I would give everything and there would be nothing that I wouldn't do for him. Maybe my expectations are too high, but I don't want to settle anymore.

Azim was top of the scale attractive—physically. He was thoughtful, caring, and wanted to get to know me on a deeper level. What I did not want to do was make the next man pay for what the last man did. So, if this was a chance to get what my heart desired, then I had to be intentional and present. I looked down at my watch and just grabbed the first thing that I touched and put it on.

The evenings in Bedford were warm enough that I could have chosen to wear something a little more adult, but I chose some palazzo pants, a nice pink v-neck t-shirt, a light green sweater, and a cute pair of sandal wedges.

When I arrived, Azim was standing by the door. He looked *so* good. There was very little on the Earth hotter than a dark skinned man wearing white. As I walked closer to him, I realized that his dark lashes made his eyes seem like they were the main attraction and the rest of his face was just a part of the show.

"You look beautiful, Bella."

"Thank you. I wasn't sure what to wear."

"You chose comfortable and that makes sense. Are you ready to go inside?"

When we entered, I was shocked to see that it was a full art museum. I am not sure what I was expecting, but this was definitely not it. There was a mixture of paintings, sculptures, and photography. I knew that I loved Bedford, but this place was quickly becoming exactly what I was missing in my life. The music nor the lights were intrusive to my brain. I found myself walking up to random people and talking. For just a moment, I wondered if I was really an introvert. I hadn't even noticed that Azim was standing on the other side of the room watching me. I made my way to his side.

"I'm sorry; I got so lost in the art. This place is amazing! Thank you so much for sharing it with me. I drive past here everyday on my way to work and would have never guessed this was here."

"The evening is not over."

"Oh? Where are we going now?"

He smiled at me and held my hand without saying anything. We walked further back into the building and he opened a door. Inside of the room were tables, a bar, and a stage. Next to the stage was a live band and if I thought that I was in a utopia before, I was now in heaven. We walked in and he led me to a table that was closer to the stage than I would have liked to be, but I was in such a good mood, I was not willing to trade that feeling in for anything negative. Painted on the brick wall behind the stage was *Euphoria*.

He pulled my seat out and made sure that I was comfortable before he sat down next to me.

"Are you hungry?"

"I could eat," I said, realizing that I could not remember if I had eaten. "But I don't know if they have anything that I can safely eat here."

He smiled again. "I was told that everything that they serve is vegan, gluten-free, dairy-free, and it sounds like, taste free. You should love it." He laughed.

"Very funny." I looked around to see if there was a menu close by. I could not contain my excitement at the idea of having a menu that I did not have to worry about.

"I think that the menu is only on the QR code. A lot of restaurants here did that during the pandemic and just never went back. Printing menus can be expensive."

"Not to mention they are major germ catchers." I added.

He looked up and squinted at me. He took out his phone, scanned the code and then handed me his phone.

I scrolled the menu and didn't even become overwhelmed by all of the options. I was too focused on finally not having to worry about the repercussions of being glutened.

"See anything?" He asked.

"Everything. I literally want to try everything."

"I could order the entire menu for you, but I am sure that the other people in here would like to eat, as well." He joked.

"You are just full of jokes this evening." I noted that he was super relaxed and playful which was not a side of him that I had seen before. "I think that I want the *Facon Berger* with bleu cheeze," I scrolled to the sides, "Oh my goodness! I have to try the sea salt sweet potato fries. Are the helpings big?"

He laughed at me. "I am not sure. I am usually at my own restaurant. I just recently heard about this place."

"What are you getting?"

I handed him the phone and he took only a few seconds to find something. Before he could share with me, our waitress came to the table.

"Hello, my name is Melisa. Would you like to order or do you need some more time?"

"No, we are ready. She will have the *Facon Berger* with bleu cheeze and a side of sea salt sweet potato fries. I will have a garden salad."

"And what would you like to drink?" She did not look at me.

"I am going to assume that you have no real alcohol here so a bottle of your finest moscato." She began to walk away when I stopped her.

"I only want water, please."

She looked back to him for confirmation and then walked away.

"You don't drink?" He questioned.

"It happens so rarely that the only answer is no."

"Is there a medical reason?"

"No. Just my personal choice."

"I see." He looked at me like there had to be a reason that I did not drink. Surely he did not think that everybody in the world liked the taste of alcohol.

The band began playing music and the room brightened softly with the candles that were surrounding the stage. Music takes me to another place and this music was so verbal that each note spoke to each one of my senses in a different way. I opened my eyes after I realized that they had been closed.

"I'm glad that you are enjoying yourself."

"This was a much needed surprise."

In the middle of our silence, a man came to the stage.

"We 'bout to get started. Now look, I know who y'all came to see, but we ain't there yet. We got some up and coming artists to warm the stage up for your boy. So sit back, relax, and enjoy all the love that is coming through the wind. Hang tight, we'll be starting in a bit."

I leaned over to Azim, "It's not a comedian, is it?" We were sitting way too close to the stage for a comedian.

"No, tonight is poetry. From my understanding there are different types of performances each night."

I nestled back into my chair and threw my hands to my sides, "They're geniuses."

The food arrived before the show began and I melted into the plate. Had I not been told that there was no meat involved, I would have never known. I had been wrestling with the idea of electing the plant-based lifestyle and this place just cast the winning vote.

Chapter Fifteen

I don't think that you can be an English professor and not have a love of words—well, at least you should. People would be amazed at the type of music that I listen to because it is so contradictory to my personality; but if my layers are really pulled back, it would not be that big of a surprise. I love words. I love music and when those two worlds collide with a full spectrum of literary devices on display, well then you have truly found my weakness. My playlist is all over the place. The best way for me to describe it is that I fall in love with the sound of synergy not artists. I am always looking for *the sound.* Even though I can not encapsulate into words what *the sound* is, I can tell you that it undresses me and leaves me naked covered only in emotions, feelings, hopes, and dreams.

When someone takes the time to convey their innermost perspectives and does so in such a way that you are allowed into their experiences, that is art. This whole evening was art. The poets were so raw and real that on more than one occasion I had to stop myself from crying. When I am in spaces that are neurotypical, I feel like I am always looking into a dirty mirror, but when I am around my people, I don't just see myself, I feel seen.

The host came back to the stage and the band started playing Anthony Hamilton's song, *Best of Me* softly in the background. "Ok, we know that you have been waiting for your mans to come to the stage and bless us. He was working out a word just for you tonight. Noone has heard it. Matter of fact he told me that he hasn't even rehearsed it. So, without further ado—Strokes."

The lights had already been dim, but the house grew darker and one lone light shone in the middle of the stage. A few seconds later, a man walked slowly to the microphone. The room was so quiet that all you could hear were the sounds of your own heart beating.

When he lifted his head and began to speak, I was frozen–it was Kamar. What had the host called him? Strokes? Without introduction he let the words flow from his mouth like melted chocolate:

>*"When you see an image*
>*And you know that you have seen God in it*
>*And it*
>*Imprints on your soul and flows out of your hand*

From the wrist

To

The

Tip

Right down to the print

Uniquely scripted and the the mold was shattered

To serve as a witness to the one who was

Beaten and battered

The kind of bruises that either change your character or

Or create it

Neurologically or physically these

Kind of bags make change

Not always for the better but hope

Lies in lines that blur as they rearrange

The way that you breathe

The purer the high

The higher the flight

But no bird gets exempt

From the trauma of the night

The same hand with the power to hurt

can heal in an even fight

We tussle

Relying on the past like a trained muscle

Flexing for foes

Whose whole treasure nose

The best way to sniff out a legacy is to beef with a bot

Or the industry

When you can duplicate it

Because you have been replicated

And the fortune is like celluloid dust

Get back in the tv before you have a problem with us

You want to be down as long as down takes you up?

You're a friend, you're a fan with half of the cause

But your half was adopted so you don't

Really feel it at all

You're just mixing words and calling it art

IF your goal is to sail

Float on

But an artist's custom eyes is because he has a story to

tell

He knows how much red makes black and blue

And that white can never erase brown

He knows the best piece never makes it to the wall

Because the holes will never let it stand

And be presented

Until a bloody path reveals the bloody mask and the

Projects are bought and not rented

A real artist doesn't pour out; he pours in

A real artist doesn't pour out; he pours in
A real artist doesn't pour out; he pours in
And he does it again and again and again
Until his heart tells him to stop
Been waiting my whole life to fall back in love with hip
hop"

I don't think that I even breathed the entire time that he was performing. There was so much that I wanted to just pick apart and delve into the corners of his mind and discuss. Had he been looking at me the whole time? Surely not, but maybe because I was sitting in front of him. Of course it could have been because I was a familiar face in the room. I felt like I was in a trance. My brain was racing but also trying to stay in the moment while replaying every word that he said.

"I have one more for you." I swear this man was only looking at me.

"I penned this one a few weeks ago. I was taking in the atmosphere and the hand of God walked past me and blessed me by breathing in the same space that I was borrowing."

No one said anything. They all just nodded as if they already knew what he was talking about. I looked at Azim, who I had completely forgotten was there, and he could not have looked any more bored.

"Are you ok?" I asked him

"English was not my favorite class. I was more into math and science."

I was confused by his response then I realized that he was trying to tell me that he didn't understand a word that had been said.

"Do you want to leave?"

"You look like you are really enjoying this."

"No worries. I drove."

"So, you would stay?"

"Probably just until this set is over."

Azim turned his head toward the stage and whispered, "I'll wait for you."

Then Kamar's voice broke through my thoughts.

"This next one actually does have a title. It's called Miss Understanding.

Love

Hate when you learn to

Love

The hate because it's in you

Find yourself and a mission that weighs less than hurt

When you're under the dog

And looking eye to eye

The people battle with you

Until you pass the sky

You're either a legacy or a villain

There aint no in between

When I am rising in the dark

Yall got me

Until the sun break then

Illuminati

I'm too dark for my brother to brag of my win

When my victory was rooted in the

Story of my skin

But birthed of the flames

My brother turned his back

Because he feels attacked–

His elevation ain't changed

So to be power

Fully

I gotta take him out

Cutting off my water

to spite the drought

Make it make scents

To smell what he's cooking

And forget about Flint

Light it up

Pass the buck

Make a dollar

When a difference would do

They say that to be woke is to be sleep walking

But we won't ever cross Jordan

If we only keep talking

One had her head

And the other held her heart

But the trauma of a mistake that she couldn't let go

Made them impossible to tell apart."

I do not think that I have felt that seen in my whole life. Don't get me wrong, Thuy knows me, but there are times when it is impossible for her to truly understand me. So how does he?

No one clapped or snapped or cheered when he was finished. The audience just got up and began to leave. I really wanted to stay and talk to Kamar, but I also didn't want to be rude to Azim.

"You are really into this kind of stuff." He said it as more of an observation than a question.

"Well, I did choose to be an English professor. It is a part of the job."

"I cook. I get it. You love what you do. We will just have to get you to try different things, yes?"

"I am always open to trying new things, but I like what I like."

"You can't read all day and then do this all night. There are other ways to have fun. We can go hiking next weekend."

"I'll be honest, hiking is not on my bucket list."

"You'll enjoy it." He said as he dismissed my protests.

Chapter Sixteen

As we got up to leave, I thought that I saw Kamar from the corner of my eye, but when I turned around to make sure, he was gone.

"Are you looking for someone?" Azim looked around the room.

"No, I thought that I saw one of my students." I lied.

"I've always wondered how teachers got a chance to be normal people when they can run into their students outside of work at any time."

"It can be challenging to say the least. When I taught in public school, I never taught in the area where I lived for that very reason."

Once we got outside, Azim walked me to my car. I couldn't stop thinking about Kamar. I had no idea that he had that much talent in him or that he was so profound. Every word that came out of his mouth seemed to undress me from the inside out. How could he have known so much about me? Surely he wasn't stalking me? Stalking me? Really Bella?

"Here I was trying to find a place with food that wouldn't kill you and it seems that I just brought you to the one that is going to steal you from me."

"I'm sorry, what?" Had he noticed Kamar looking at me?

Azim laughed. "The food. It looks like you have a new favorite place to eat."

I was so relieved that he didn't realize what actually had my attention. And, why was I thinking about Kamar when I was out on a date with a man who has made his intentions clear from the beginning? He wasn't talking in riddles and playing head games. He always made sure that I was safe and cared for. Azim was so attentive and he made me feel like I was the only person in the world. So why was Kamar monopolizing my mind?

"My second favorite place to eat." I smiled at him.

"That makes me happy that you would lie like that to spare my feelings." His amusement only lasted for the briefest of seconds and then his face became very serious. "I have to be honest. I don't know how to do this. I spend most of my time in the restaurant and the other time with my family. I don't know if I am making my intentions toward you clear." He gently lifted my head with his hand, "or perhaps you are just not interested."

"Azim, before I moved here, I was in a horrible relationship and it ended very badly. Nothing that you are feeling—my distance—is about you. It is about me making sure that I am doing what is best for me and not rushing into another relationship simply because it's available."

"I see."

"I know that there is no way for you to know how hard this transition has been for me, but I do appreciate that you have been so patient."

"So you are not ready to be in a relationship, that is fair. We can be in a pre-relationship." He laughed.

"A pre-relationship?" I asked.

"Yes. We date. We eat. We spend all of our time together. You dream about me. I dream about you and then we get married next summer, yes?"

His unseriousness broke the uncomfortable heaviness of the moment. "You are a great man, Azim Patel."

"Yes, yes I am and I am going to be an amazing husband."

I got in the car and drove back down Central with the intent on going home, but I remembered that I needed to pick up some oat milk and cranberry juice. I was not in the mood to fight the crowds at the neighborhood supercenter, so I drove to TiTi O's hoping that she was still open.

I pulled into a parking space on the side of the store and noticed that Emilia was sitting at one of the cafe tables. Her face glowed in streaks of tears under the dim light.

I got out of the car and walked over to her. "Emilia, are you ok?"

She looked up to me with swollen red eyes, "Oh, hello Dr. Hawkins." She attempted to stop the flow of her tears by dabbing her eyes with the corner of her jacket. I reached into my purse and pulled out tissue and handed it to her.

"Do you need to talk?" I sat down in the chair across from her trying to let her know that I had time for her and that I was truly invested in her well-being.

"There is so much going on Dr. Hawkins. I don't even know where to start." I didn't say anything. I picked up her phone and added my contact information. I wanted to give her space to choose where to begin but also let her know that she could talk to me on her own time. "It's school. It's home. It's—"

Before she could finish, Ashlee walked up. She looked irritated and rushed to Emilia's side.

"What's wrong?" She said while looking at me.

"I'm not sure." Ashlee's protective nature reminded me of Leah and how she was always willing to fight anyone for me or Thuy.

"I'm ok. I just got a little overwhelmed. My mom is still sick, but she won't go to the doctor and I think that it is serious."

"If it was serious, she would go to the doctor. Stop worrying. I was just in there. She said that she was going to lay down and had me make a warm cup of tea. She will be fine." Ashlee said.

"Wait. What do you mean that she is *still* sick? What are her symptoms?" I asked.

"She's been crazy tired and I even hear her throwing up in the middle of the night."

"How long has this been going on?"

"I think that it was right about the time that I started college. At first, I thought that it was just her being nervous about me going to school, but it's not like I moved out. I am at home every night."

"They are really close. I have been trying to get Emilia to be my new roomie, but she won't leave home." Ashlee interjected.

"Ashlee, I told you that moving out doesn't make sense. I work here and there is no way that my mom can afford to hire someone else. Now with her being sick, I am probably going to have to work even more. You are already here everyday helping out."

Ashlee didn't even attempt to hide her disappointment. The early twenties were such a crazy age. You are legally an adult, but there was so much kid in you that you don't always understand that the world is not always going to work out the way that you want it to. Besides, are you even alive if you are not bathing in narcissism at that age?

"What if I talk to her? See if I can get her to get checked out?" I offered.

Emilia's eyes lit up and she bolted out of chair and hugged me so tight that I almost fell out of my chair.

"Thank you Dr. Hawkins! My mother trusts you."

"She trusts me? She doesn't even know me."

"It's really not you, it's Semper. Our dog. Semper likes you."

"Well she hates me." Ashlee added.

"She doesn't hate you Ashlee. She can just tell that you don't like her."

"I don't like any dogs." Ashlee said.

They both laughed. Emilia had cheered up enough for me to go in and get the things that I needed. When I walked in, I was surprised to see TiTi O sitting down behind the counter.

"Are you ok?"

She looked up at me as if she didn't know who I was for a moment. "Sweet Bella. I am tired. It's been a long day."

"Are you sure that's all? You don't look well."

"You sound like my Milly. All the time she says, 'madre go to the doctor,' Go to the doctor for what? I am old, old people get tired."

"First of all, you are not old. Second, I don't think that it is a bad idea for you to at least get a check up. It would make us all feel better, if you did."

"Fine. I go to the doctor, he say I sick, then what?"

"Well, if you are sick, then we can find out how to get you healthy again, but if you wait too late, we might not be able to do so."

"Dr. Bella, I go. I go tomorrow. For you and Milly, I go."

"Thank you. You know, you are one of the reasons I love Bedford so much."

"Azim, that is why you love Bedford." She patted my hand and winked at me. "He is a good man, Dr. Bella."

Although I felt like I could have an honest conversation with her, I didn't want to burden TiTi O down with all of my issues, so I just smiled and paid for my things.

"I am going to come to see you tomorrow so you can tell me what the doctor said, ok?"

"Ok, Dr. Bella. I go."

I couldn't wait to let Emilia know that I was able to get her mother to agree to go to the doctor, but when I got outside and walked around the corner, she and Ashlee were gone.

"The attention spans of youth." I said as I opened my car door.

"I guess that makes you young at heart."

I looked up and Kamar was standing by the cafe table. "I didn't expect to see you until I got home."

"I was headed home and I saw your car. I don't have a tracker on you, Bella."

"I know."

"I didn't expect to see you tonight." He said without looking at me.

"I know. I'm sorry about that."

"Don't get me wrong, I loved having you there, I just–"

I interrupted, "I know."

"So, you still think that I am killing people?"

"I never said that Kamar."

"You didn't have to say it."

"I don't think that you are killing people. I don't *know* you."

"You do know me."

"How?"

"You know you."

"Kamar, I want to know *about* you. This feels alot like mind games and I am way too old for that."

"You think that I am trying to play with your mind?"

"I think that you spend so much time trying to prove to me that you see me, that you are intentionally trying to stop me from seeing you."

"What do you want to know, Bella?"

"Everything."

"Fair enough. Starting where?"

I thought for a moment. Was this really what I wanted to do? There was no way for me to have this conversation and not be more confused than I already was.

"Why does Sheriff Bailey think that you are a murderer?"

"Ok, we are going to start there, huh?" I nodded. "When I was younger, I didn't make the best of decisions. I spent a lot of time trying to be like everybody else and I got involved with the wrong people and I was around when a lot of foul stuff went down." He stopped talking and looked at me. "Mind if we sit in the car for a minute?"

I unlocked the car and we got in. I wasn't sure if he didn't want to accidentally be overheard or if he wanted to make sure that I would listen to the end of what he had to say.

"I don't have stories about an absent father or an abusive mother. I made choices, but I always had options. I made choices that my parents didn't live to see me regret. My senior year in high school, my father was doing his best to stay connected to me, but I wanted the streets. My grades were never in danger and I could have gone to any college that I wanted to. I was provided for. I was protected. My father was the mayor of Bedford at the time. He had been in some form of politics my whole life and maybe living under the microscope was what got to me."

My father was not the mayor, but I knew too well what it was like to be constantly watched by over zealous church members that had their own ideas about who I was supposed to be.

Again, he paused to look at me. I just listened. "I could have gone to private school, but I wanted to be normal. I couldn't see that what my father was—who my father was was the manifestation of generational tears, protests, and deaths. I thought he was soft because he didn't talk about the struggle. I didn't realize that he was in the trenches of the struggle and in a position where he was not just fighting racism he was also having to fight black people, too."

I am not sure why, but I started the car and just drove around town. Listening to him talk and seeing parts of the town that I had not paid attention to, gave me an opportunity to become a part of his story. I wanted to see it from his perspective.

"Pull over there. Can we park for a minute?" He asked.

We pulled into the abandoned car wash. He got out of the car and walked around. When he reached a spot near the last stall, he stopped walking. I got out of the car and walked to his side.

"The 90s were a crazy time. We used to park all up and down this road playing music and dancing and just hanging out. This new cat had been in our school for about a year and we got tight right away. He was like my brother. I didn't have many friends. Folks was scared to hang out with the son of the mayor, but Jeff wasn't. He saw something that I had not seen. I had a trouble pass that other black folks didn't have. One Sunday, we were out here on the strip like we were every Sunday evening and I saw this girl that I had really been diggin'. So I went to talk to her. She was over there." He pointed across the street. "I had been gone for a few minutes and then I heard cars screeching and breaking and people screaming. Bullets were flying so I pushed her to the ground and laid on top of her. She was shaking. I think I was, too. I didn't get up until I heard the sirens."

A car drove by and Kamar stopped talking. I knew that he was trying to tell me something, but I also was starting to think that this was not the smartest or safest idea that I have had.

"You could smell it." He looked at me to see if I understood. "Smoke and death. Fear and hate. Blood. The blood was running. It wouldn't stop. My boy Jeff had been hit in the head. Probably was gone before he hit the ground." A tear refused to fall from his eye so it just sat there growing.

I wanted to reach out to Kamar but I didn't know how he would respond. He didn't seem to know that I was there anymore. It was like watching someone watch a movie that only he could see. I could only wait for the time when he let me in.

"I rode with Jeff, so I had to wait until my parents came to get me. They had told me not to go, but I went anyway. I just knew that they would be mad, but when they got there. It wasn't me on the ground so they–." His voice trailed off. He went silent then he coughed. "I stayed until they picked up the body. I wasn't going to let him be alone. Jeff—it was just Jeff didn't have—his mom worked a lot and his brother had just left for college. Jeff was a kid that was trying to figure it out, you know? He talked about all of the stuff that he was going to do for his mother and buy her. He did what he felt like he *had* to do. He couldn't go to any college after school. He didn't play sports, so he thought his future was limited. I knew some people and I introduced him. I thought, at the time, that I was helping him, but instead I ended up killing him."

It took a minute for his words to sink in.

"Kamar, your friend made a choice. His choice had consequences. You didn't kill him."

"Did he really have a choice? He had a mother that worked three jobs just to make sure that he almost had enough to eat. He had a brother who was so focused on getting out of town that he didn't have time for him. He had a father who had been in jail his entire life. What choice did he have? He only wanted—what I had."

"You didn't cause any of those things to happen. I don't know why Jeff couldn't have been born into different circumstances, but he wasn't. That had nothing to do with you."

Ignoring my rationale, he continued, "After the fact, I was messed up. Like really messed up. I couldn't get over seeing all of that potential laying on the ground. So I did some things. Jeff's family blamed me for his death. His brother swore that I pulled the trigger. It made it difficult for my pops to keep his position and he stepped down to try to save me. I was in and out of trouble so much that—I didn't know that my mother was sick. She died. I cleaned up for a while, but when my father died a year later, I finally understood what I had had but it was gone."

"I cannot imagine having to deal with that much loss at such a young age."

"Even though I was not the best version of myself when they were alive, my parents made sure that I had options available once I wanted to get help. I've never really had to want for anything, and none of that has ever replaced the hole in my heart."

"Justin—Sheriff Justin Bailey is Jeff's brother, isn't he?"

"Yep."

"He is not going to look for another suspect, is he?"

"Nope."

Chapter Seventeen

When I finally got home, all I wanted to do was get in the shower and then in bed. I was so overstimulated that I felt like I was about to crash out. All I wanted was answers about Dr. Bisson and it seems like that was unraveling the whole town's legacy. Why was I doing this anyway? Why was I inserting myself into an actual criminal case? But, considering what Kamar told me tonight, how could I not? If it is true that Justin blames Kamar for his brother's death, then he is not going to stop until he ruins Kamar's life. How can I sit back and let that happen?

I left a trail of clothes and worries all the way to the bathroom. A shower was not going to be enough; this was going to have to be a soak-in-the-tub kind of night. I got my candles, my music, and let the water run just full enough that it would not rush on to the floor but still be high enough that it would cover me up to my neck.

My mind was racing. There was something that I was missing, but my thoughts wouldn't settle down so I could figure it out. There were too many emotions. Too many moving pieces. Moving pieces! That's it. No matter how big a puzzle is, all of the pieces have to come together to present one picture. I've done this a million times. I just needed to identify all of the corners and work my way in, but first I had to flip over the pieces so that I could see what I was dealing with. And, as my mother had told me; there are no coincidences, just set time and due season.

I got out of the tub, dried off, and slid into my pajamas. These were my 'could pass for lounge–but-suitable-for-outdoors wear pajamas; it's the weighted calming effect of the texture that relaxed me. When I got to my bed, I knew that there was no way that my mind was *not* going to focus on the puzzle trap that I had just created. I promised myself to only plot out my next steps and not to go down the 'who's involved' rabbit hole (I would save that for tomorrow). I reached to turn the light off and the phone rang. Of course it did.

I didn't look to see who was calling, "Hello?"

A frantic Emilia wept violently as she tried to talk to me in between sobs. "Dr. Hawkins?"

"Emilia, what's wrong? What happened?" I instantly sat up and turned the light back on.

"Can you come—-come, please?" She begged.

"Where are you?" I was already slipping on my tennis shoes and thanking God that I had chosen to sleep in something that didn't need to be changed.

"Home," was all that she was able to manage to get out before her hysterics took over. I feared that something had happened to her mother, but I didn't want to initiate another trigger if that was not the issue.

"Ok. I am on my way. I am only about five minutes from you. Stay on the phone with me, ok?"

"Ok." She sounded like a baby. My heart was breaking and I didn't even know why.

I *might* have driven faster than the speed limit to get to her and I was fully aware that if there was a deputy anywhere near that I would quickly be getting a ticket. When I pulled up to the store, I went in and Emilia was sitting at a cafe table near the coffee shop door.

"Emilia." I said quietly. She was nervously rocking back and forth and shaking her head.

She didn't respond to me. She just kept whispering, "No, no, no, no, no, no, no, no, no, no."

I looked around the room to try and figure out what had her so scared. It wasn't until I walked behind the counter that I saw Titi O. I ran to her to see if there was a pulse hoping that she had just fainted, but she was gone.

I slipped my phone out of my pocket and called 911. I was sure that I was the only person, or at least the first person that she had called. Within minutes, the paramedics and fire department had arrived.

There was nothing that I could say to Emilia, so I just let her cry on my shoulder until she felt that it had been enough.

"What do I do now?" She asked.

"There is no way that you have to figure that out tonight."

"I can't stay here."

"Get what you need and come home with me."

"Really?" I nodded. "I don't know what to get."

"Let's just lock up. I'll put a sign on the door. I've got clothes and anything extra that you would need. Don't worry about anything."

The short ride to my apartment was quiet and took a few minutes longer than the drive over. I didn't think that this was the time for small talk or to try and find out how she was feeling. She just lost her whole world. Just the thought of what life would be like without either of my parents would completely crush me and I was at the age when losing a parent was inevitable. When we pulled into the parking lot, I didn't move until she was ready.

"What am I supposed to do now?"

"You don't have to figure that out right now."

"I never knew my father. He died before I was born. My mom did all that she could to make sure that I never missed him. I don't even know if he had family."

"Is there somebody in your mother's family that you would like for me to contact for you."

"You know, I don't even know. How crazy is that?" She started crying again, "and now I can't ever ask."

"Let's go inside." A shower and goodnight was not going to fix her broken heart. There were no words that I could say that and there was nothing that I could do that would ever make this pain end for her.

When I opened the door, Emilia looked around.

"You sleep in the living room?"

"Not really, but yes. This" I pointed around me, "is my bedroom. I write over there. I exercise over there. I eat over there—the few times that I do eat at home."

"It's different, but I like it."

I laughed. "Well then you will love sleeping in my closet." I showed her to the room. "Whatever you need should be in the little closet over there—towels, clothes, toiletries—whatever. That is my storage. The bathroom is right in front of the door. Take all of the time that you need.

I am going to make up your bed and it will be ready for you when you get out."

She didn't say anything, but I could see the pure exhaustion in her eyes. She wasn't a baby, but now that she was all alone, there was such an innocence around her that it was heartbreaking. Even when I hid from the world, I knew that when I was ready to rejoin life, that I had my family and my sister. Speaking of my sister, I am so glad that I let her convince me to put a sleeper sofa in my closet.

I pulled out the bed and put fresh linens on it. I wasn't sure if Emilia had a charger with her for her phone, so I plugged up one that had multiple types of connections.

"Maybe a bottle of water and some tissue." I went into the kitchen and grabbed a bottle and a small trash can. I typically don't like people in my personal spaces, but I was feeling something. What was it?

When she came out of the bathroom, she looked into the room and turned to me and whispered, "Thank you," and closed the door.

To Thuy: Sissy are you asleep?

From Thuy: Almost, but not enough to cuss you out. What's up?

To Thuy: I won't be at work tomorrow.

From Thuy: I was going to ask how the date went, but now I know.

To Thuy: No.

From Thuy: Ugh! Guess the cobwebs are still intact.

To Thuy: You remember my student Emilia?

From Thuy: Friend of your weird ass assistant?

To Thuy: Stop. Yes.

From Thuy: What, Kamar kill her, too?

To Thuy: No. Stop saying stuff like that.

From Thuy: Awww when y'all getting married?

I walked out onto the balcony and made sure to close the door behind me. I called Thuy.

"You don't ever call people. I'm on my way." Then she hung up.

Yes, she had a foul mouth and yes she was infinitely smuttified, but there was not one person on this earth that I would rather do life with. When I was a child, I hated being an only child. Don't get me wrong, my parents were and are the best, but I hated being alone sometimes. Sure, I had other friends from time to time before but it wasn't until God gave me Thuy that I found out what having an actual sibling was like.

The smell of coffee drew me out of my thoughts and into the present.

"Scoot over." Thuy climbed into the seat with me and cuddled under the blanket. "It was supposed to be getting easier for you here."

"None of this is your fault."

"I know. I just know how much you deserved to finally have some peace."

"It hasn't been all bad. I love having you so close to me."

"And Azim. Oh yeah, how did the date go?"

I let out a big sigh and sunk deeper into the seat. "That was even worse."

"What happened? Did the fine man try to tickle your cookies?"

"Which one?" I questioned.

"Ooooooooo, wait a minute." She sat up and looked at me, "What we talkin' bout now? Y'all in a throuple? I shouldn't have had you watching that damn Shameless."

"You are so unnecessarily nasty. No, Azim had planned out this thoughtful date. He found a restaurant that was gluten-free and plant-based. Girl, there was art, live music, and poetry."

"Damn and *you* still came home with panties on?"

"Focus." I redirected.

"I'm just saying that *that* sounds like he was tapping into things that you like. What happened?"

"Don't get me wrong, I was totally enjoying myself and then the headliner—apparently the one that everybody was there to see came on stage."

"Don't tell me. It was your little serial killer, wasn't it?"

"Well, in the artist world, he is known as Strokes—and *do not* say one word." Thuy closed the invisible zipper over her mouth while poorly hiding her laughter. "Not only did he get up on that stage and completely take the air out of the room, he had written the poems for me."

"What? You got three of the finest men in town making complete fools of themselves and you haven't even let them smell it?"

"No seriously, what happened to you?" I took a long look at her. "Why are you like this?"

"Fun? I was made this way. I promise God be laughing at me."

My laugh turned into stillness. "Her mother died."

"I figured. I didn't know that she had been sick."

"Me either. When I met her, she seemed anything but sick.

"That poor girl."

"I know. She could have been in shock and just couldn't remember, but it seems like she doesn't have any other family."

"What in the hell? That is so fucked up. She is not alone, she has us. What do you need from me?"

"I really need you here, sis. I don't want her to be alone right now either. I'm feeling feelings and I don't like it."

"Sounds like I just moved in for a while."

"We could go to your house if you want. Three women and one bathroom sounds like a very bad 90s sitcom."

"We definitely cannot go to my house. You don't need to know me like that."

My laugh turned into a deep yawn. "I need sleep."

"You need rest, but sleep will do for now."

Thuy pulled me up and pushed me to my bed. I got on one side and she got in on the other side.

"Do you need another pillow?" I asked her.

"Nah, I'll just take yours when you start snoring. And don't be farting under the covers either. I'm not trying to die from vegan gas ass-bombs."

"I do not snore."

Chapter Eighteen

Thuy never ceases to amaze me by how caring she can be. By the time that I awoke the next morning, she had called the university to tell them that we would not be in and cooked breakfast.

"Good morning, babe." She said in an unusually bright voice.

"Good morning sissy." I looked towards the closet door. "Is she up yet?"

"I think so. I didn't want to bust in on her."

"I get it, but we really should check on her. She was pretty out of it last night."

"I'm ok." Emilia came into the kitchen and sat next to me on the barstool. "Surprisingly enough, I am also hungry. Is that bacon? Emilia reached into my plate and took a piece.

"Oh you are living dangerously, sticking your hand in that heffa's plate." Thuy warned.

"She's fine. Now you on the other hand. Who knows where your hands have been."

Emilia laughed. "I love yall's friendship."

"Girl, that is my sister." Thuy corrected. Emilia looked at me for confirmation. "I'm pretty sure when someone comes into the bathroom while you are using it that means that you have surpassed friendship and can only be considered family."

"To be clear," I added, "it was Thuy that came into the bathroom because she couldn't wait to tell me about some fine man that she had seen earlier that day."

"Whatever heffa." She laughed and looked at Emilia. "You and your friend, Ashlee, seem pretty close, too."

"We are, don't get me wrong, but we are not *that* close. I have only known her for a year."

"I do remember you telling me that. So, how did you meet?"

"It was really strange. I was rushing around at the coffee shop and trying to get to the university, but it seemed like the more that I tried to get things together, the more that they fell apart. Right before it was almost too late for me to get there, Ashlee walked in to buy some tea. I thought that it was weird that she asked for tea."

"Why?"

"The young people here have been drinking coffee since middle school and it is even rarer for young people to come in specifically for tea. That's what started our conversation and then she told me that she was a chemistry major at the university. So we ended up going over together. She helped me get all of my stuff together."

"That's what friends do." I said looking at Thuy.

"Yeah." Emilia agreed, then seeing that Thuy still had food left on her plate, she asked, "Are you going to eat that?"

Thuy raised her left eyebrow and pushed the plate over to her, then looked at me. "Go for it."

"You guys finish eating and I am going to get dressed." I said.

"Sounds like a plan. I'm going to run home for a little bit and grab a few things.

When I got out of the bathroom. Emilia had washed the dishes and was sitting on the bed scrolling through her phone.

"Do you mind if we go back to my house?"

"Are you sure?"

"Yes. Can't avoid the inevitable. Besides, I feel like I need to be handling business. I'm sure that they are going to want to know where to send the—my mom."

"Of course. Whatever you need."

As we drove down the street, I caught myself looking to see if Kamar was around. I wanted to see him and talk to him, but I also did not want to encourage his pursuit. I didn't know how I felt about him, but I did finally know that I was not ready to be involved with anyone.

It didn't take us long to get to the store.

"Do you mind parking in the back? It's easier to get to our apartment that way."

I drove around to the back and wondered how I didn't notice the driveway before. I have always been praised for my ability to notice small details, but since I had been here in Bedford, it was like that part of my superpowers had been blocked.

We got out of the car and walked up the stairs. Emilia unlocked the door and stopped walking. At first, I thought that she saw something, but then I realized that she was overwhelmed with the reality that her mother was never going to be there again.

"I have never had to do something like this before."

"I haven't either, but I did help my friend Leah prepare things when her sister passed away. Did your mother have a life insurance policy or a Will?"

"I am pretty sure that she did. Now, where that stuff is, I don't know."

There was a light tap on the door and then Thuy walked in.

"I totally forgot to tell you that we were going to leave."

"You know I keep my eye on you at all times." She tapped her phone. "So what are we doing?"

"I need to find my mother's life insurance policy. I vaguely remember her telling me that, but when you are younger, you don't want to hear that kind of stuff."

"Trust me, you do not want to hear it when you are older, either." I said. For a brief moment, I imagined having to do this for myself and I instantly had to stop before I became hysterical. My parents were my everything.

"There is a box under my mother's bed. I have never looked in it. I wonder if she kept it there." Emilia led us into her mother's bedroom. It was much smaller than you would expect for the master bedroom and very minimally decorated. The only character in the room was pictures of Emilia.

"You were a super cute little girl. So much personality!"

"You don't know the half of it. I didn't get in trouble, but I was not an easy child. I always had questions. I think that my mother sometimes avoided me." She laughed for a moment and then opened the box.

"I wonder." Emilia said to herself.

"You wonder what?" Thuy asked.

Emilia hurriedly looked through the contents of the box, she slowed down when she found pictures. Each picture initiated a different expression from her, but none that matched the excitement that she had when she began.

"What's wrong?"

"Oh nothing is wrong, I was just hoping to see pictures of my mother when she was younger or of her with her family." Her voice trailed off. "You know, I have never even seen a picture of her when she was pregnant with me. I really wanted to see that."

"Ohhhhhhhh." Thuy sang as if she was actually learning something different than what Emilia had shared. She locked eyes with me and our sisterly communication confirmed our suspicions.

As Emilia continued to look through the contents of the box, she noticed an envelope. She opened it and poured out a small key.

"A key?" Emilia looked both disappointed and curious.

"Did your mother have a safe deposit box?"

"Maybe." She thought a little bit longer, "Yes, yes she did. I can't remember why she told me that, but maybe that is where the life insurance policy is."

"Do you want to go to the bank or do you have other things that you need to do here?"

"I just need to pick up a few things. Are you sure that you do not mind me staying with you for a while?"

"You can stay with me as long as you need to."

"Are you sure? I don't want to be a burden, but I also don't want to be alone right now."

Thuy hugged Emilia. "You are not alone. You are now a part of our crazy crew."

We all laughed until we heard a door slam. Thuy was the first one out of the bedroom and I do believe that she had her hand in her pocket for a reason. I followed and Emilia was close behind me.

"Where have you been?" A very angry Ashlee yelled.

Thuy took her hand out of her pocket and looked at Emilia. "She is definitely talking to you."

Before Emilia could answer, Ashlee continued her rage-filled questioning. "I have been calling you and texting you all night. Then I came by here this morning thinking something horrible had happened and I find you here just laughing and having a good time."

Emilia's lifted spirits began to plummet and I made my way to her side.

"Ashlee. I understand that you were worried about your friend, but she doesn't need this kind of pressure right now." My delivery was a little more stern than I had intended but I was not liking the way that she was talking to Emilia.

"I'm sorry. My mind was all over the place and I forgot to charge my phone. My mother died last night." Emilia explained.

"You didn't charge your phone?" Ashlee questioned.

Both me and Thuy found her focus on the phone and not the fact that her best friend's mother had just died was more than strange.

"Kind of hard to remember your phone charger when your whole world just got shook." Thuy interrupted.

Ashlee looked at Thuy and softened her tone, and walked closer to Emilia.

"I'm sorry. I was up all night thinking that something had happened to you and my emotions were all over the place." Then she looked from Thuy to me, "I promise that I am not insensitive. I don't have any family here and I guess I just overreacted."

"Did you hurt yourself?" I asked, referencing Ashlee's slight limp.

"A little. I tripped up the stairs. I guess I was moving too fast."

"Well, we should be going." Thuy said ignoring Ashlee. When Thuy was done with a person, she was done.

"Going?" Ashlee looked at Emilia.

"I have to get things in order for my mother's—I need to make arrangements."

"Oh, I can help with that. What do you need me to do."

"There is nothing for you to do right now, but perhaps Emilia can call you as soon as we have some things in place."

"Of course." Ashlee smiled, put her head down, picked up her bag, and walked out of the apartment.

There was an uneasiness in the room wrapped in a silence that was hard to discern. Although Ashlee went way overboard with the protective best friend act, Emilia seemed to not want her around.

"First stop, bank?" Thuy broke the air.

"That is what I was thinking, too." Emilia responded.

"Do you have everything that you need for now?" I asked.

Emilia looked around the apartment. "I think so."

She looked so sad and so alone that it was very easy to see how she looked as a child. She was only twenty-something, so technically, she was still a child. There was so much that she still needed a mother for.

When we got to the bank, we had to wait for the manager to check the account and to show us where the box was. Once the manager had verified her identity, she led us into the vault. The manager opened the box, gave a sympathetic look, and left us to the room.

Emilia walked over to the box and opened it. Inside the box was a letter, insurance papers, and a small gold ring.

"I don't remember this," Emilia said as she held the ring up. She handed the ring to Thuy and then she opened the insurance envelope. "I think this is what we needed."

She handed the envelope to me and I looked over it briefly. From what I could tell, her mother made sure that she would be financially secure for many years to come. While I was reading through the terms of the policy, Emilia was staring at the other envelope.

"What is that?" Thuy asked.

"It looks like a letter. I don't recognize the address. It's to a woman named Maria Estrella in New Orleans."

"Are you going to read it?" Thuy asked.

"You think I should? It seems personal."

"What if Maria is a relative?" I suggested.

"That's possible, I guess. I was always given the impression that we were alone. It would be wonderful to find family."

Emilia pulled the letter out. It had yellowed from time and the paper was fragile. The ink was almost completely faded in some spots which made it difficult to read:

Maria,

You have been nothing but a light in my life. I still feel guilty about involving you in this mess of a life that I have. It is just not going to work out for us. I hope, in time, that you will not just be able to understand, but to forgive me. I owe it to my wife to work it out. We gotta try. While we were separated, my daughter was born. I didn't even know that she was pregnant. My place is with my family even if my heart is with you.

Love Always,

Diego

"Damn, Diego, that is fucked up." Thuy said.

"Is there a return address?" I asked.

"No. Could you mail stuff like that? Emilia asked.

"I'm not sure. Can you see a date on the envelope?

"A little. It looks like August 26, 2005."

Emilia sighed and put the letter back into the envelope. I knew that she was thinking about her mother, but my brain was now onto another puzzle. It would be so great to find Emilia's family for her. Thuy looked at me and knew exactly what I would be doing tonight.

Chapter Nineteen

When we left the bank, we went to the local funeral home where Emilia had told the hospital to send her mother's body. We were unaware that there was a release form that needed to be signed, so Emilia signed the form, gave the director a copy of the policy number, and then went back to my apartment.

We all fell into different chairs around the room. We hadn't done much, but that didn't stop the day from being extremely draining. Right before I started to snore embarrassingly loud, I got up and tapped Emilia on the shoulder.

"Go lay down. I am going to go to the university and get a little work done. I should be back by the time you wake up. If you need me or if you need anything, just text me."

She looked up at me, her eyes heavy, and whispered, "Thank you," before she drifted off to sleep. I smiled at her and closed the door quietly behind me.

Thuy was curled up in my bed and it would have been an exercise in futility to try and wake her up. I grabbed my keys and left. While I was walking to my car, I couldn't help but smile but instantly felt horrible. I was smiling because I really love having Thuy and Emilia at home with me. I didn't realize how lonely I had been. By virtue of nature, I am somewhat of an introvert, but when I am with *my* people, they get all of me. I yearned to have that safe space around me. It had been a while since I felt safe. I had been hurt, I had been lied to, I had confused, used, and dumb, but not safe.

"I love seeing you smile. That doesn't happen enough." Kamar was standing by my car.

"I agree. Why didn't you come upstairs?"

"Where is Azim?" Kamar raised an eyebrow.

"He is not upstairs, if that is what you are asking."

"Why isn't he upstairs?"

"Because he doesn't know where I live and I have not invited him."

"You still don't trust your instincts, huh?"

"Kamar, I-"

"I get it."

"No, no you don't. I just need some space to figure some things out and now with everything going on with TiTi O and Emilia. I'm just all over the place."

"What about TiTi O?"

"Oh that's right. You may not know. She passed away the other night. It was the night that you and I drove around."

He pulled his hand out of his pocket and held mine. "I didn't know. Is Emilia ok?"

"As good as can be expected." I looked down at his hand and noticed a bandage on his arm. "What happened? Are you hurt?"

"I was building a big canvas frame and it got away from me. I'm fine. It's just a few scratches."

"A few scratches? It was bad enough that you put a bandage on." I tried to examine his arm to make sure that he was ok, but he stopped me.

The right side of his mouth turned into a slightly mischievous smile. "I am fine."

I looked at him and thought that fine was not a good enough word. He was beyond fine. I quickly gathered my thoughts.

"Ok. I have to run a few errands. Can we talk some time? Like really talk? I want to get to know you. I don't want to hear what others have to say about you. I want to hear what you have to say about you."

"I get it."

"Ok. I have to go. Maybe this weekend?"

He nodded and walked down the sidewalk.

Normally when I was in for a drive, I would have an audiobook playing, but today, I just wanted to be in silence. There was so much information swirling around in my head that I felt like I was missing something. It was like all of the pieces had been poured out on the table and I had flipped most of them over, but I still was missing something.

When I got to my office, I was surprised to see that Ashlee was at her desk.

"I didn't expect to see you here."

"I wasn't sure if you were going to make it in and I wanted to make sure that your students had the information that you sent over."

"That was very thoughtful of you." I noticed that she was avoiding looking at me. "Are you ok?"

"Yes." She paused. "Well, no. I feel so helpless. I know that Emilia needs me and I don't think that I helped very much this morning. I was just so worried about her."

"She knows that. It is just a lot going on right now. Give her some space. She will reach out to you in her own time."

"When I met Emilia, she was so full of life and funny and the only thing brighter than her smile was the sun—until he came along."

"He?"

"Emmy had a crush on this older guy. I don't know, maybe it's a dad thing. At first it was just a little flirting, but then she started becoming more distant from me."

"They started dating?"

"That would have been fine. Everybody dates but he just did stuff that made no sense."

"Like what?"

"Like when we would be at his spot, he would ignore her or act like he only remotely knew her. I saw their texts one day. I wasn't trying to—that's when I found out that it was more than a crush."

"When you say older, are you saying old enough to be her father?"

"I don't know if he is old enough to be her father, but he definitely has lived more than she has. I think her mother found out and forbade her from seeing him anymore."

"How did he take that?"

"He started dating someone else and pretty much rubbing it in her face."

"I am sure that that crushed her."

"She was angry. She started throwing things and blaming her mother and the new woman that he was dating. She promised to pay them all back for ruining her life."

"Hurt will make you be irrational for a moment. Sometimes, we say things that we don't mean." I explained.

"You are probably right." Ashlee looked down at her phone, "Gotta go. Class. Do you need me to do anything this afternoon?"

"No. Take the rest of the day off." I noticed that one of her nails was broken. "Maybe stop by the nail shop." I joked.

Ashlee looked down at her hand and immediately put it in her pocket. "My books were slipping out of my arms and I was trying to catch them and not spill my coffee."

"Been there, done that."

"Ok, Dr. Hawkins. I will see you tomorrow?" She asked.

"Yes, I will be here."

I watched her leave the office and then I realized that I had not put my things down and my arms were feeling it. I went into my office to do some research. I still wanted to find Dr. Bisson's family, but that seemed to be less and less the focus as the new things were so much more pressing. I had a student who was more than likely pregnant, living in my home and currently all alone because her only family member just died. Not to mention this thing with Azim and Kamar.

Kamar—I almost forgot about the fact that he had a Sheriff who was going to make sure that he went away for a murder that I am absolutely positive that he did not commit. Or, did he? He could have, but why would he have? What did I really know about him? Nothing. I know nothing about him except that he talks in riddles and oral puzzles. Maybe that was what it was. Maybe I was attracted to him because he was a puzzle—a living breathing walking double entendre. Or, maybe I was attracted to him simply because he is so fine. Ugh!

Why couldn't I fall for the guy that was open with his intentions? Why couldn't I fall for the guy who was stable and was in a healthy family? Of course, my ex-husband was a lawyer and he came from an amazing family, too. Was that it? Was that what was bothering me about Azim? Kamar was always telling me to trust myself but since I was not very happy with "her" right now, I didn't trust her either. I moved to Bedford to start over and to find myself, but all I found was puzzles and more problems.

I sat down at my desk and purposely did not look out of the window. "Where to start?" I opened up the notebook that had all of my information about Dr. Bisson that I had left on my desk. "She worked for CPS. Then she published a study about a case that involved a child. There has to be an abstract on the study."

I think that I crashed every scholarly journal search engine there was. When I was about to give up, I found a news article that caught my attention. It was about a woman named Maria Estrella.

"Could that be the same woman who Diego wrote the letter to?" I opened the link. The article was about a woman named Maria Estrella who was a custodian at CPS and was among the missing people from the hurricane. How absolutely heartbreaking that so many people were lost and there are no answers. According to the article, Maria's family looked for her. Her house was intact, but she was nowhere to be found. Because there was no information, she was assumed to have died in the storm.

"She had family!" That was the best information that I had found. "There has to be some information on the family if they were vocal about looking for her." After ten minutes of searching, I had found out that Maria's mother and father had dedicated the rest of their lives to finding her–their only child. Unfortunately, they both had died years later.

"Dead end." I whispered to myself.

"What's a dead end?" Sheriff Bailey was standing in my door watching me. "I didn't mean to startle you. You must not have not heard my knock."

"I did not." I closed the laptop and my notebook. "How may I help you, Sheriff Bailey?"

"That was very formal. Let me guess, you are mad at me?"

"I am not mad at you. I just disagree with the direction that your investigation is going."

"That is because you don't know all of the information that I know."

"I know that you cannot blame someone today for something that you think that they did a long time ago."

Sheriff Bailey's smile faded.

"Dr. Hawkins. I commend you for being a caring person, but do you think that you know everything about Kamar?"

"I never said that. I just don't believe that he would have had a reason to kill Dr. Bisson."

"Well, what about Opheila Alvarez?"

"TiTi O?" I laughed out loud. "Are you kidding me? I was there. Her daughter told me that she had been sick for weeks. There is absolutely no way that you can blame that on him! Besides, he was with me."

"Oh really?" He raised an eyebrow. "One word. Flexillin."

"Flexillin? What is that?"

"I'm glad that you asked. Flexilin is a synthetic chemical compound that maintains the flexibility and durability of paint. It is particularly valued in the art and construction industries for its ability to keep paint supple, preventing cracks and maintaining a fresh appearance while the paint dries."

"It is used in paint?" I half-asked, half-stated nervously.

"Yes."

"So that means what?" I pretended not to understand that he was telling me that Kamar would have access to the chemical and a reason to have it.

"Nothing, by itself. Want to know what the symptoms of ingestion are?"

I tried to hide my nervousness, "Sure."

"Initial symptoms of Flexilin poisoning include mild nausea, fatigue, and headaches. Over time, symptoms progress to severe abdominal pain, jaundice, and organ failure. Sound familiar?"

"I will admit, this is not my area of expertise, but what I do know is that all of this, while it may be true, is only circumstantial."

Oddly, he began to smile as if he had anticipated that I would not be convinced by his 'evidence.'

"Let me tell you a story. There was a young boy who loved his mother feverishly. He was his mother's heart and joy, but she suffered from depression. Many people speculated that her depression was initiated by the weight of being married to a wealthy and powerful man who also had a hard time keeping his penis in his pants. She ended up being admitted into a mental hospital and unfortunately died there."

I wasn't sure where the story was going, but a knot was growing in the pit of my stomach so big that it was making me lightheaded.

"The boy was too young to know what was going on. A couple of years later, his father remarried. That woman was good to the boy. He loved her immensely. She filled the hole in his heart. But one day, while he was at his mother's favorite coffee shop, he overheard the owner and a few other women gossiping about how his step-mother had been having an affair with his father and that that relationship with her *friend's* husband had led to her mental breakdown and ultimately her death."

"How horrible. I still don't see how this makes—"

"The stepmother died suddenly and shortly after this. Want to know what her symptoms were?"

"Are you telling me that Kamar poisoned his stepmother?"

"Am I? No, but what I am telling you is that there is a strange pattern going on here."

"Even if this is true—and I am not saying that it is, how does this include Dr. Bisson?"

Sheriff Bailey stood up, smoothed his pants out, and headed towards the door. When he got to the door, he turned around.

"Want to guess who his mother's psychiatrist was?"

I didn't answer. I didn't need to.

"Dr. Hawkins, your friend is in custody now and he will be charged, tried, and sentenced. Consider yourself blessed that he hadn't gotten to you yet."

Chapter Twenty

My head was spinning. Was there any way that I did not see that I was falling for a killer? There was no way. I had to trust myself. I had to trust my spirit. Had I trusted my spirit before I got married, I would have never been in that situation.

I opened my laptop. What was I missing? Yes, Kamar could be guilty and he definitely had motive and opportunity, but what was I missing? Who was I missing and why did it seem like everything went back to New Orleans? My need to figure this out wanted me to hop into my car and drive to Louisiana.

I was in an information overload. I needed a break. I decided to pack up my things and get something to eat. I drove on autopilot to Azim's restaurant. I had had very little food at home and it was about time for Thuy and Emilia to wake up; both of them were definitely going to be hungry.

When I walked into Azim's restaurant, I was shocked to see Cory there.

"I didn't know that you worked here?"

"I just started. Is it just you today, Dr. Hawkins?"

Before I could answer, Azim came over.

"I've got it from here, Cory."

Azim moved to the side and extended his hand for me to sit where I wanted.

"I expected to hear from you way before now."

"I know. I wanted to come by and tell you why I haven't texted you. Emilia is staying with me. Her mother died last night."

"What? Is that why the store has been closed? Why didn't she call me?"

"Why would Emilia have called you?"

"You know Bedford is a pretty close-knit community—especially the business owners."

"Right. Well, like I said, she is with me and I have been dealing with that."

"I wasn't aware that you two were close enough for her to be living with you." He had a strange look on his face and seemed to be avoiding eye contact with me.

"I wouldn't say that we are close, but she is a student of mine and she was in need."

"Is that smart?"

"Is *what* smart?" I was becoming a little frustrated with the barrage of questions that I was getting from him.

"Having an unstable student staying with you. Troubled people have a way of misinterpreting kindnesses."

"Unstable?"

"Well, maybe that is not the right word. Troubled is better, yes?"

"Is there a reason that you don't want me to help her?"

"No. I just want you to be safe. Forget I said anything." He changed the subject. "You came for food, yes?"

"I did, but not to eat here. I want to take it home."

"Ok. Look over the menu. I'll send Cory over to take your order. I am trying to put the final touches to my office."

Azim walked over to Cory and a few minutes later, Cory was at the table to take my order. While I waited for the food, I intentionally silenced my mind. I needed to be clear so that I could start putting the pieces together correctly.

I am not sure how long I was sitting alone. It wasn't until Cory brought my order that I realized that I was sitting at the same table that I had been sitting the first night that I had come to the restaurant. That had been the first night that I had seen Ashlee and Emilia. Actually every time that I had been at the restaurant, they had been there. Azim was right about one thing, Bedford was a small place and with all of this tragedy, it was getting smaller by the day.

When I got home, Thuy was sitting at the table working and Emilia was sitting at the breakfast bar eating an apple.

"I've got food!" I said when I opened the door. Emilia met me at the door and took the bag out of my hand. She looked at the bag with frustration, "You went to Azim's?"

"I did. Do you not like the food there?"

"It's ok."

Thuy, who noticed everything, gave me a questioning look. I made sure to be in a space that was out of Emilia's sight, and mouthed, "I'll explain later."

To which she mouthed, "The fuck?"

I laughed, but Emilia was so involved with the chicken leg that she was demolishing that she didn't even notice.

"I saw Ashlee today."

Emilia finally stopped eating. "Oh. She was probably still pretty mad at me, huh? What did she say?"

"I don't think she was mad at you. She just wanted to make sure that you were ok. I, too, have a crazy friend who is way too emotional and is—"

"Quick to cut a bitch behind my sister." We laughed. "What did ol' boy say," Thuy thought for a minute. "'I might tell a joke, but I won't never tell a lie.'"

"And that is why I love you." I blew a kiss in Thuy's direction.

"Yeah." Emilia contemplated. "Have you ever been real cool with someone, but then for some reason, you just didn't want to be around them anymore?"

I thought about Azim and Kamar. Even though the evidence was stacked a mile high against Kamar, I wasn't convinced that he could kill anybody. And, as good as Azim had been to me, something inside of me just wasn't feeling him.

"I completely understand. You don't have to figure it out right now.

"Thanks." She returned to her plate and then she yelled, "SEMPER!"

It took me a moment to realize what she was talking about.

"What the fuck is a Semper?" Thuy asked.

"She's not a what, she's a who." I explained.

"My dog. Where is Semper?"

Withouthesitation, we left the apartment, got in the car and drove to Emilia's store. When we arrived, there was crime tape around it and Sheriff Bailey was walking around.

"What is going on? Why is there crime tape around my mother's store?" Emilia asked the sheriff.

Sheriff Bailey looked at me. "Ms. Alvarez, we have reason to believe that your mother was murdered."

"Murdered? How? By who?"

Sheriff Bailey again looked in my direction. "We have a suspect in custody."

"Who is it?" She begged.

"Kamar Prosper."

"Kamar Prosper? The painter? Strokes? Absolutely not! He loved my mother and she loved him. They talked for hours. He was even painting a mural in the coffee shop for my mom."

The Sheriff shot me a knowing look.

Oblivious to the sheriff's look, Emilia continued her protest. "There is no way that he would have done that."

Thuy was looking at me and I could tell that she was questioning why I wasn't responding to the news.

"We have strong reasons to believe that he may have heard some information recently that caused him to act."

"I don't care what your evidence says. There is no way that he did this!"

"I assure you Ms. Avarez, we are going to pursue every lead that will answer all of these questions that we have."

"What about my dog?"

"Your dog?" Sheriff Bailey asked.

"My dog is missing. Her name is Semper."

Sheriff Bailey took out a notepad and wrote that down.

"We will look for her. She may have seen the perpetrator."

"I don't understand. How was she killed?"

"She was poisoned."

"Poisoned? Is that why she was sick?"

"How long had she been sick?

"I don't know. Right around the beginning of the semester. Yeah, I remember worrying about her having to work while I was in class."

"School has been in for a few weeks. Is there anyone else that works here with you or that has access to your store or home other than Mr. Prosper."

"No. My mother was super private. I can ask my friend, Ashlee if she saw anybody new. Sometimes she would help out with the cafe right before we were about to go somewhere, but she wasn't around that much. She only started helping a few weeks ago."

"Where does Ashlee live?"

"It's not too far from here." Emilia opened up her phone. "I can airdrop you her contact information."

Once Sheriff Bailey received it, he promised to keep her updated on the investigation.

We all looked at each other and purposefully did not say a word until we were back in my car.

Thuy was first. "He ain't do that shit."

Emilia was next. "There is no way he did it."

"I don't think that he did it either, but somebody is going to a lot of trouble to make it look like he did."

"Ok, it's time for you to do that autism spectrum disorder detective shit. This is serious. They are trying to fry that man."

"You don't know how serious it is." I looked at both of them. "They are also charging him with Dr. Bisson's murder."

Both Thuy and Emilia yelled, "What?"

I nodded and turned off the car once we were back to the apartment.

The color was draining fast from Emilia's face. "This is too much for me, right now."

"Of course it is. You need to rest. I'll put some water in your room. Go lay down."

She got out of the car and went upstairs.

"Sissy, you have been trying to figure all of this out by yourself, haven't you?" Thuy was not happy.

"All I wanted to do was to find Dr. Bisson's family, but the more that I dug into her life, the more that I found out that all of this mess was connected and that something very bad happened in New Orleans."

"Ok. Run that shit back from the beginning.."

I looked around like there may have been a chance that someone was listening to us.

"At this point, everybody is a suspect. We have to look at *everyone* with fresh eyes."

"Everybody but Emilia, right?"

"Everyone."

"I know you fuckin' lyin'! You mean there is a chance that she killed her mother and you got us living with her?"

"When I got to my office today, Ashlee was there."

Thuy curled her lip with so much disgust that she didn't have to tell me that she didn't like her. "Why was that weird bitch there?"

"Thuy." I pleaded.

"Ok, my bad. Why was your weird ass assistant in your office when she knew damn good and well that you was not going to be at work?"

"Point noted. Well, anyway. She told me that Emilia was in a relationship with some older guy. The guy pretty much was using her and ignored her when they were around other people."

"I can see that. She is pretty but she does *give* stupid."

"Point noted. According to Ashlee, TiTi O did not approve of the relationship."

"Did they break up because of the mother?"

"See, that is what I don't get. Ashlee said that her mother made them stop, but she also said that the man was flaunting some new woman around in front of Ashlee."

"I ain't seen her around anybody but Ashlee."

"Me either."

"Oh, maybe it's Dr. Abebaw."

"Girl, stop."

"I can see it now," Thuy said, mimicking Dr. Abebaw, "Emilia, I celebrate you for having some good-good."

"No ma'am. You will not." I said laughing uncontrollably.

"Right outside of the gates." Thuy said about her eternal home after she died.

"Focus." I thought for a moment. "The only other man that I had seen her around was Azim."

Thuy stopped laughing. "Well, he *is* older."

"And both she and Ashlee were always at his restaurant—until lately."

"Oh shit, Bella!"

"That would explain a lot, actually."

"Like, why you haven't been able to seriously date him?"

"Yeah."

"Ok, but that scenario makes Emilia a love-sick killer and answers for the mother's death, but what about Dr. Bisson?" Thuy questioned.

"Right. Our killer has to have had motive and opportunity for both murders because there is no way that they are not related."

"You said something about New Orleans being a link to everyone. So we need to find out who has ties to New Orleans."

"Right." I reached into the backseat and pulled out my laptop and notepad. "Dr. Bisson, of course. TiTi O seems to have some connection."

"This shit getting good!" Thuy nestled down in her seat. "How is she connected?"

"Remember that letter from Diego?" Thuy nodded. "I was looking for information on Dr. Bisson and ran across an article about a missing custodian that worked at CPS named Maria Estrella. Can't be a coincidence."

"Mom said that there is no such thing. Remember? The fullness of time and due season is all we got. So, hell yeah this shit is related. And quite fucked up, I might add."

"Maria was assumed to be lost to Hurricane Katrina. Apparently, after the storm, no one heard from her, but her house was intact."

"She could have tried to escape and got swept away on the road or something. So how is Maria tied to TiTi O?"

"Good question. The article said that Maria's mother and father tried to find her until they died. So maybe there are pictures of her family. Might be a sister."

I opened the browser on my computer and searched for images of Maria Estrella, CPS, and missing in Hurricane Katrina. When the pictures came up, we both were stunned.

"Oh shit! That's Ophelia. TiTi O is Maria!" Thuy said.

"Ok. Wait a minute. Wait a minute." My mind was racing at top speed. "So she faked her death?"

"But did she really? She just left without telling anybody. Moved and changed her name."

"What would have made her do that?" We both looked at each other and said, "Diego!"

"Ok, so Maria and Diego was getting it in." Thuy recounted. "Then he left her and went back to his wife—who had just had a baby that he didn't know about." Thuy thought for a minute. "That's easy, you don't leave, you kick his ass and then blow up his spot."

"That is what *you* would do, sissy."

"True. So why didn't she do it? You know, blow up his spot? Not literally, but figuratively?"

I talked myself through the possibilities. "Maybe" I thought deeply. "because she was pregnant, too?" I suggested.

"Right! And ain't no way she was going to be able to explain to her parents how she got a whole baby and not a piece of a boyfriend in sight."

"Good gravy!" I yelled.

"Would you just cuss, already?"

"Focus. When I met TiTi O, Dr. Bisson was there and she had said that she thought that she knew Ophelia. She absolutely did know her. They worked together–"

"At CPS!" We both said.

"So did TiTi O kill Dr. Bisson?" I wondered.

"That's a good question. Why would she kill her?"

"What would have been worth killing the woman for? She could have easily brushed it off. She could have even gone as far as to say that Maria was her relative, but there has to be a reason that she didn't want her to know that she was Maria."

"Was Dr. Bisson married to Diego?"

"That would be a good reason, except that Diego's wife couldn't have known Maria. Remember, the letter said that he didn't know that his wife had had a baby."

"Right."

"I think that we need to take a break. This is a good start. We are close." My brain was starting to hurt.

"Are we agreed that we do not think that Emilia killed her mother?"

"Yes."

"But what about the Azim thing?"

"Now *that*," I paused and took a deep breath. "is a good question."

Chapter Twenty-One

It wasn't until we got upstairs that I remembered that I had told Emilia that I would put some water in her room. Just before I opened the door, I heard her talking. All I could hear was her side of the conversation:

"The food was good, thank you."

"I haven't said anything to anyone."

"No, I do not know what I am going to do."

"I know that I can't stay with her forever. I don't want to be alone."

"So you would rather me go home to the place where my mother was killed than to stay here?"

"What about with you?"

"I know that we are not together, but you don't care what happens to the mother of your child, really?"

"I really hate that I ever met you."

After that, all I heard was sobbing. I decided it was not a good time to take the water into the room.

"Was she on the phone?" Thuy asked.

"Yes." I hushed Thuy and pointed to the balcony. Once we were out there, I made sure to close the door.

"I think that she was talking to Azim."

"Eeeewwww. He really knocked up that little girl?"

"Sounded like it."

"And to think that he kept having me come there and he was rubbing it in her face."

"I slit tires." Thuy informed me.

"Focus. We have to protect her from him."

"Could he have killed Ophelia when she confronted him about Emilia?"

"If you would have asked me that an hour ago, I would have said no, but anybody low enough to play with the emotions of a child and then throw her away once she was pregnant, is capable of anything."

"Now I have to slit throats, too?" Thuy threatened.

"Focus. Someone killed her mother." I reminded Thuy.

"What if there were two different murderers?"

"That could work. Ophelia killed Dr. Bisson."

"And Azim killed Ophelia."

"But how did the killer know to use the same poison?"

"Right. So it had to be someone who wanted both of them dead."

"And someone who has ties to New Orleans."

The sliding glass door opened and Emilia came out with us.

"Feels good out here."

"Yes, it does. How are you feeling?"

"Better. A little hungry, though."

"There should be some stuff left from earlier—"

Emilia's guilty look let me know that there was reason to finish that statement.

"It's my time to get food. What y'all want?" Thuy asked.

"Whatever you decide." I responded.

"I'll be back in a jiffy."

Emilia and I stayed on the balcony.

"Let's talk, Emmy."

She smiled. "My mom used to call me that right before I got in trouble."

"Well, you are not in trouble, but there is some serious stuff going on and we need to talk about it."

"I'm pregnant." When she realized that I was not surprised, she continued talking, "it's Cory's. I know he is a jerk. Well, I know that now, but when we first met, he was so sweet."

My head was doing that spinning thing that it does when information is rushing in. "Cory from class?"

"Yes. I broke it off with him when he started flirting with that girl in class. Then he started sending all of this weird stuff to my phone. He was more concerned about you finding out about us than actually what was going on with this baby. He refused to believe that I just didn't want to be with him anymore. He actually thought that I was seeing someone else."

"Does Ashlee know about Cory?" I was confused.

"Does she know about him? She was one of the reasons that I broke up with him." A knot was forming in my stomach again.

"Emilia, how much do you know about her?"

"Not much to be honest. I know that I originally thought that she was from Texas, but then one day she mentioned seeing me on tv when she was in New Orleans."

"Oh my God! That's right, Ashley is from New Orleans!"

"Yes she is. Why?"

"What did your mother say about her?"

"She didn't like her at first, but that is how she is with anyone that I meet."

"Why didn't she like her?"

"It was Semper. Semper hated Ashlee. As a matter of fact, if either my mother or I was not in the room, Semper acted like she wanted to attack her."

Emilia jumped up as if she had been electrocuted, "Gotta go pee. This going to the bathroom thing is getting crazy."

I smiled, "It gets crazier."

I sat with my thoughts. It had to be Ashlee. But why would she have killed these women? She had a definite dislike for Dr. Bisson. Maybe she didn't like Ophelia. Why would she make me believe that Emilia was dating Azim when she knew that that wasn't true." I held my head in my hands. "Emilia! That had to be it. She wanted Emilia all to herself so she was trying to get me to kick Emilia out, but how did Dr. Bisson fit into all of this?

I went back inside and prayed that God would lead me to what I needed to know. I was still missing something. I typed Dr. Bisson's name in the search engine again and a review of the study came up:

The case was about a child who had been taken from her parents. The girl had shown violent episodes that started after she witnessed a woman kidnap her baby sister from the shopping cart at a local grocery store. The father notes that the child and he were extremely close and that she would often accompany him to work in his construction business. The parents had trouble in their marriage and had separated. During that time, the child became very protective over her newborn sister and had, on more than one occasion, threatened the mother. After the sister's disappearance, both parents were found in the home and had been poisoned. The child was taken into custody and was to remain in a treatment facility until the age of eighteen. At that time, it would be determined if she could be released into the general population.

I did one more search. If the child had been kidnapped, surely the parents would have done at least one interview. I had to be sure before I told Emilia what I had found out. I didn't find any videos until I added the name Diego. And, there it was. She was young, but the picture was definitely Ashlee or as the ticker-tape said, Diego, his wife

Illiana, and their daughter Lillibeth and they were looking for their daughter Elizabeth.

"Oh. My. God." was all I could say.

"Oh my God, what?" Emilia laughed.

"You need to sit down."

"You are scaring me."

"I know." I took a deep breath and tried to figure out how I was supposed to tell her this story. So, I just did it.

"Ashlee is my sister? My mother kidnapped me? My sister killed Dr. Bisson and my mother?"

We were both in a state of shock.

"Wait until I tell Thuy."

"Where is she? She should have been back by now." Emilia asked.

"Thuy talks a big bad game, but knowing her, she is probably out buying baby clothes."

"It's a little early for that."

"We need to go to the police station. Let's take everything."

Emilia picked up the letter and the little ring fell out again. This time, she closely inspected it.

"There is an inscription. The writing is tiny. Oh my God."

"What is it?"

"It says '*to my baby sister, Lizzy.*' My name really was Elizabeth. I had a mom and a dad and a big sister that loved me and my mother—and Maria took me from them because she was mad? She broke my sister into pieces."

I went to her and hugged her. The fact that she was not actively losing her mind was a miracle in itself.

"Come on Emilia."

We walked out of the door and down to the car. There was a note under my windshield wiper blade:

You stole my sister, so I am taking yours.

I dropped the note.

"Dr. Hawkins, what's wrong?"

"Your sister—Ashlee, she has Thuy. I think she is going to kill her."

"No, this has to stop!" She thought for a minute, "I know where she lives, let's go there first."

"You can't go."

"She won't hurt me."

"I can't risk anything happening to you or that baby. I will drop you off at the police station. Tell Sheriff Bailey everything that we found out and then meet me there."

"She might try to hurt you."

"I'll be fine. Just get there as soon as you can."

Emilia texted me Ashlee's address and I dropped her off. I drove to Ashlee's house, but there was no one there and it was dark.

"Why did we think she would be here?" I started to panic.

"God, I need your help. Please don't let anything happen to my sister."

I sat and thought for a little bit. All of the pieces were there I just had to think. I opened up my phone and began looking through my photos. That's when I saw the panoramic picture that I had taken the night Dr. Bisson was killed. I expanded the view and looked at the picture closely–hoping that I had gotten a shot of Kamar in it. I didn't, but I did get Ashlee in the window of Dr. Bisson's office!

I immediately texted the picture to Sheriff Bailey with a message telling him to zoom into the window.

Before I closed my phone, I remembered that Thuy and I always shared our locations with each other. I had her location! I pinned it and sent it to the sheriff and told him that I was on my way to get my sister.

Thuy's location led me to a small building on the outskirts of Euless. It was more rural than city, but if you didn't know that it was there, you would have easily missed it. I got out of the car, and I was careful not to make too big of a sound when I closed the door. I didn't know what I was walking into, but I was going to do whatever I could to get my sister out of there even if it meant losing my life.

The sun was setting fast and I would not have much natural light left, so I had to decide quickly how I was going to get in the building. It didn't take me long to find Thuy once I was inside. I immediately ran to her and removed the tape from her mouth. Her wrists and ankles were bound with plastic ties that were extremely tight.

"Are you ok?"

Before she could answer, I felt a heavy sting to my head and then everything went dark. When I woke up, I was connected to Thuy and Ashlee was walking back and forth in front of us.

"You just wouldn't stop. I did everything to stop you, but you wouldn't stop. You kept putting your nose in things that had nothing to do with you." She stopped and looked around as if she had heard something. Then she walked out of the room.

"I wonder where she went."

"Can you move, sissy?" I asked.

"Not really."

"I am so sorry." I apologized.

"For what? That heffa is crazy. This is not your fault." In true Thuy fashion, she cracked a joke, "Weird ass is going to kill us, ain't it?"

It took everything in me not to laugh.

Ashlee came back into the room and began pacing back and forth in front us. Something had spooked her. After a few minutes, she calmed down.

"I do have one thing to thank you for, though. If you had not told me that Dr. Bisson was here, it would have messed up everything."

I didn't know if I should let her keep talking or if I should start asking questions. I decided to interact with her hoping that that would give the police time to get there.

"Why?" I asked.

"Why? Why?" She didn't even try to control her anger. "Dr. Bisson was the reason that I was locked up all of those years. She told the courts that I was unstable and that I should not be allowed to enter society."

"That was harsh. Didn't she realize that you had no choice?"

Startled by my statement, Ashlee stopped walking. "No, I guess not. What else was I supposed to do? That bitch Maria took my Lizzy and my parents were so busy fighting that they didn't even realize it."

"How did you find her?" Thuy asked.

"I was scrolling through videos one night, and there she was. She was much older, but I knew it was my baby sister, my Lizzy. She had won a writing competition. I took one look and I knew that that was my baby sister Lizzy."

"Why didn't you tell her who you were?"

"I couldn't. Not at first. I wanted her to get to know me again. I knew that if she just got to know me again, she would see it. She would know that we were sisters and she would leave that woman."

"Neither one of you deserved any of this. You should have been able to grow up in a happy home and with loving parents."

"Yeah, well."

She stopped talking again as if she had heard something. I needed to distract her just in case it was someone to save us.

"What did Dr. Bisson do?"

"Huh?" She turned back to me. "Oh yeah. Her." Ashlee's eyes became small and filled with hate. "She had me locked up like an animal. She said I was dangerous. She said that I was—crazy." She turned her head abruptly and then back to me. "I AM NOT CRAZY!" She yelled.

"Of course you are not. You are hurt. What Maria did to your family was unthinkable. How did you do it?"

"I gotta thank you Dr. Hawkins. When I first saw her before school started, I thought that she looked familiar. So I followed her. I didn't know that bitch was in Bedford. She could have ruined everything." She stopped talking. "I said that already." When she found her train of thought again, she continued, "So I changed my major so that I could be seen in the building regularly, but I never let her see me. I needed to watch her. When she saw me at the cafe and recognized me, I knew that she had to go. Then, Lizzy mentioned that Dr. Bisson came into the cafe regularly for the tea. That's when I knew."

She was talking in circles and I knew that I had to refocus her. "You poisoned her tea."

"Sure did, but I couldn't risk doing it slowly like I was doing Maria. Before Maria, my dad and I were always together. He owned a construction company and he taught me everything! I learned how to lay sheetrock. I learned how to wire a house, and I learned–."

"How to mix paint." I finished her sentence.

She smiled with so much pride that it made her look like a crazed clown.

"I like you, Dr. Hawkins." She put her head down. "You are a good person."

"I think you are a good person, too. Your sister will see that. We can talk to her together and tell her your side of the story."

"You would do that for me?"

Before I could answer, her head jerked to the side, again then she got up. I looked at Thuy and mouthed to her that we were going to be ok. Out of the corner of my eye, I saw a pair of eyes looking at me from the dark corner.

Suddenly, Ashlee stormed into the room and grabbed me by my neck.

"You brought someone here with you, didn't you?"

"No—I swear." I said as I fought to breathe, but her grip was so tight that I could feel my air slowing down. Thuy tried to kick at her, but she couldn't reach her.

"You are just like all of them. Nobody else is taking my sister from me!" Her grip around my neck became so tight that she was almost able to interlock her fingers.

The next thing that I heard was a loud growl and then Semper was ripping Ashlee to shreds. She locked on to Ashlee so tight that I could hear the bones in her arm crunching. Blood was spewing from Ashlee's arms and her face.

Sheriff Bailey ran into the room, gun drawn. As soon as Semper saw him, she let go of Ashlee and ran over to Emilia. One of the deputies handcuffed Ashley as Sheriff Bailey cut me and Thuy free.

I don't think I could have hugged my sister any tighter than I did right then. When we were done, Sheriff Bailey helped me up and looked me over. "I should have listened to you. Are you ok?" Sheriff Bailey said.

"You were following the evidence. That is your job."

"You were right about him, this time, but believe me when I tell you, Kamar is not a good person."

I looked over to Emilia, "Not now Justin. He nodded.

Emilia and Semper ran over to where we were. I bent down to pet Semper. Semper was licking my face and snuggling so much that I had to laugh. That's when I noticed that something was wrong with her head.

"Oh no, what happened." I held her head in my hand.

"When the crash-out dummy brought me here, Semper was lying on the floor. I thought that she was dead. I think Ashley had hit her or something." Thuy explained.

"Thank God she was here. If Semper had not attacked Ashlee, I would definitely be dead right now."

Because Ashlee was determined not to be mentally competent to stand trial, she was placed in a high security facility until the time when she could answer for her crimes. Considering that she spent most of her life in a similar place, I didn't anticipate that she would ever make it to a courtroom.

Emilia and Thuy had pretty much moved into my apartment full time and I was ok with that. Almost losing them was not something that I would be getting over any time soon.

"We are going to have to get a bigger place." Thuy said.

"I am way ahead of you. I found a cute little four bedroom home not too far from here. Two of the rooms are super close to each other and would make a great mommy and baby suite."

"Are you serious? You bought a house, Bella?" Emilia beamed.

"I did. We can move in in a couple of weeks, right in time for the baby bun to arrive."

"What have you decided to do about your mother's—Ophelia's store?" Thuy asked.

"I am going to sell it. I could never live there again and I don't want to run the store. Too many memories."

"I definitely understand." Thuy said.

"I decided what to name her."

"Oh really?" I was surprised because she seemed to be avoiding naming her baby. "Names are important." I said.

"I agree." Emilia said.

"Are you going to tell us or do we have to wait until Bun is in college?" Thuy urged.

"Elizabeth."

I stopped walking and looked at Emilia, "I think that is a beautiful name." I had to stop myself from crying because she didn't know why that name was beautiful to me.

Chapter Twenty-Two

After we moved into the house and life settled down. I took some time to think about my personal life. I had moved to Bedford to find myself and even though I kept finding myself in unbelievable situations, I did find out who I was. I learned that the parts of me that I was not fully in love with were uniquely tied to my gift and that I needed to embrace all of me.

I also realized that I couldn't choose between Azim and Kamar because I didn't really *want* either of them. Ok, that may not necessarily be true, but I didn't really *need* either of them. That didn't mean that we couldn't be friends and it definitely didn't mean that one day we couldn't be more, but for now, all I wanted was my sister, Emmy, and that little Bun.

"I'm not cooking." I said.

"Neither am I." Thuy said.

"I'm pregnant." Emilia said.

We all laughed and knew that that meant that we were going out to eat.

"Let's go to Azim's restaurant." Thuy couldn't even hold in her laugh.

Both Emilia and I said, "Let's not."

"Ok, ok, ok. There is a creole restaurant over there that I have been wanting to try out."

"That sounds wonderful." Emmy sang as she rubbed her belly.

"You sound super fat." Thuy mimicked Emmy's singing.

"I'm not fat, I am pleasantly plump." Emilia tried to say with a straight face.

"Girl, take your pleasantly plump ass to the car." Thuy ordered.

"I don't like your tone." Emmy faked offense.

"I'm leaving both of you." I said.

When we pulled up to the shopping center, we noticed a crowd standing on the sidewalk between Azim's restaurant and the restaurant that we were trying to go to.

"Let's be nosy." Thuy said and before we could protest she had skipped her nosy tail on over to the restaurant. We slowly followed.

"What's going on?" I asked a woman that was standing near the sidewalk.

"Not sure. I think someone got hurt or something."

Sirens filled the air and before long, the Sheriff was there along with the ambulance and fire department.

"We should go. It was probably a grease fire or something." I said.

"You just don't want Azim to come out and see you and think that you care."

"That, too." I laughed.

"Good to see you Bella." Kamar said.

I had been so focused on not seeing Azim, that I didn't even think about running into Kamar.

"Good to see you, too. You look good."

"Thank you. I think that little misunderstanding got my attention."

"It got everybody's attention."

He looked over to Thuy and Emilia who had conveniently put just enough distance between us that they could see and hear, but could not be heard.

"How is she doing?" He nodded his head toward Emilia.

"She is getting there."

"She is blessed to have found you."

"We are blessed to have found each other."

"We never got to have that conversation that you wanted to have." Kamar reminded me.

"I know."

He didn't press the conversation or the issue.

"When you are ready to have that talk. Call me. I have a phone now."

"Strokes has a phone now?"

He took my phone and put his number in it. "I even drove here." He said proudly.

"That is very interes—"

A woman's scream broke into our conversation. We both looked for Thuy and Emilia first to make sure that they were ok. They pointed to the restaurant.

"I got this." Thuy said to us as she pushed her way into the crowd.

It didn't take long before she returned with the news.

"Well, what happened?" I think all three of us asked at the same time.

"Azim is dead."

Made in the USA
Middletown, DE
03 April 2025